THE PENDEX

GARLAND REFERENCE LIBRARY
OF THE HUMANITIES
(VOL. 227)

THE PENDEX

An Index of Pen Names and House Names in Fantastic, Thriller, and Series Literature

Susannah Bates

GARLAND PUBLISHING, INC. • NEW YORK & LONDON
1981

Library of Congress Cataloging in Publication Data

Bates, Susannah, 1941–
    The PENDEX : an index of pen names and house names
in fantastic, thriller, and series literature.

    (Garland reference library of the humanities ;
v. 227)
    Bibliography: p.
    Includes index.
    1. Anonyms and pseudonyms—Indexes.   I. Title.
Z1041.B37   014'.1   80-8486
ISBN 0-8240-9501-4

Printed on acid-free, 250-year-life paper
Manufactured in the United States of America

CONTENTS

ACKNOWLEDGMENTS

In a project of this length, stretching over four years, the help given me and the interest evinced has been overwhelming. But first among all the others I must thank my parents, Charles and Elsa Church, for their continuing support, my husband, David A. Bates, for his belief in this project and the Putnam Public Library of Putnam, Connecticut, for its great help in locating some of the more unusual source texts I have used. And for suggestions and continued interest, I thank my editor.

PREFACE

"Of the making of books there is no end"; this is equally true of the making of pseudonyms to disguise the true names of authors. The reasons for this are at least as varied as the subjects of the works, but a basic reason is perhaps simple shyness on the part of the writer. Not all of us are born with a sense of destiny, particularly when it comes to presenting our thoughts and the characters we have envisioned to the reading and publishing world. Use of a pseudonym affords at least some protection to our egos and identities, and if the work is unsuccessful, we can always try again, using another pseudonym, and re-emerge on the writing world as a totally different talent. There are many other considerations, of course: political bias, sex discrimination, copyright protection—all have played important parts. A blossoming author may create a series with which, under one particular name, he is forever after identified. But what if he wants to write about something else? One way to effect the change without losing original readers is to invent a new pseudonym, thus creating a separate market for the new series, and become a successful writer twice over. In theory and in practice, the possibilities are limitless. Whole publishing empires have been founded on the abilities of a stable of half a dozen writers, writing three or more novels at once, thus creating about two or three separate books per month, and maintaining this activity over a period of years.

That is one of the fascinations of pseudonyms and house names—the indication they provide of the variety of fields in which so many authors perform. The amazing thing is that, by and large, the writers perform so creditably. Also noteworthy is the amount of overflow: the genres of fantasy, thriller-mystery and science fiction are all closely aligned and can overlap to a remarkable extent, based as they all are on a logical sub-world created by the author, and demanding close attention and sus-

pension of disbelief by the reader. Many fine stories, including
some of the great classics, are combinations of these three
genres, with overtones of sea stories, westerns or Victorian romances, for example, thrown in for good measure. This over-
lapping of genres is a primary reason for the PENDEX. Although some previous works of this type have been attempted,
each was severely limited by the type of subject matter it did or
did not include, and the definitions have been narrow at best. An
index of pseudonyms in science fiction, or thriller-mystery, or
fantasy is an excellent thing, but what happens if an author has
written in all these fields, as well as the equally viable children's
series, or western, or historical romance fields (sometimes
known as the sword-and-sandal school)? Are only his pen names
in the first three fields to be included, to the exclusion of all the
other works? And what of the combinations found in the works
themselves? A perfectly plotted mystery may also be an excellent
example of historical romance, and if it also contains elements of
science fiction or weird terror, or a plot which unfolds over a
period of centuries, then how, working in the established, narrow guidelines, does one identify such a work (two prime exam-
ples of which would be Bram Stoker's *Dracula* and William Hope
Hodgson's *House on the Borderland*)? The simplest approach
would be to ignore all such hybrids, but this is self-defeating.
There is also the problem of definition and personal taste. If an
index is to contain nothing but authors of weird terror, what
happens to Lewis Carroll, as an extreme example? Although
Carroll himself would probably have been appalled to hear it,
there are some highly intelligent readers who feel a sort of gen-
tle terror in parts of the two Alice books, simply because each is
based on the idea of an intellectual paradox carried far beyond
all logical extremes, to the point where reason and sanity no
longer have any perceptible existence. But such a definition
applies equally well to the far different Oz series by Baum, the
privately horrific world of H.P. Lovecraft, the scientific night-
mares of Huxley, Orwell and Wells, George MacDonald's
adult fantasies and C.S. Lewis's *The Screwtape Letters*, to name
only a few.

　　With this in mind, I have tried to keep my criteria for the
PENDEX as simple as possible. Granting its basis in the fields of

science fiction, thriller-mystery and fantasy, if an author has contributed a poem, short story, novelette or novel in any of these fields, I have tried to include him, and all the pen names that he uses which I have been able to verify, no matter what the subject. This standard also applies to editors of anthologies, which justifies my inclusion of two names not usually thought of in connection with literature: Boris Karloff and Zackerley. Each man was an actor in horror and comedy, each had a fine appreciation of the classic horror story, and each edited fine anthologies which are now looked upon as classics within that field. I have also used as a guideline the English language; that is, if an author has been translated into English, that justifies his inclusion in this PENDEX. Conversely, if there have been no translations, I have not included the name, simply because my own knowledge does not extend to foreign languages.

One final reason for the PENDEX should be mentioned. Some pseudonyms are identified in books of extremely small edition, now long out of print and unavailable except to the specialized collector or the most inclusive of libraries. For the most part, when any of these editions is discovered, it sells for an exorbitant price; some are no longer to be found at any price, even by search services. A number of the privately printed and distributed reference guides no longer exist in the Library of Congress: some, through sheer oversight, were never included there, despite their proven existence. When possible, I have tried to include such long-unavailable information in this PENDEX, hoping to make it once again accessible to the general collector and student.

Some of the more recent reference guides I have questioned as to accuracy, and so they have not been consulted. Some guides I would have liked to consult are now so scarce as to be almost legendary and impossible to locate; some few books, while containing much information on the popular magazines, contain no information at all on the individual writers and seem unaware that house names were ever employed. A recent privately printed volume quoted a number of sources under the heading of "Private communications." I have avoided this volume, and such a classification, drawing instead on printed sources that carry no such restriction. Also, I have tried to verify each entry in the PENDEX from at least two separate printed sources. Sometimes my own sources are a bit esoteric: after thirty years of collecting, I have been able to draw verifications as to identity from sources as varied as old letter columns, catalogues of defunct magazines, books in extremely limited edition and reference books kindly supplied by the authors themselves, all of which have been of immense value and most of which are no longer available to the general public.

Since documentation of pseudonyms is an open-ended subject at best, and since this PENDEX is largly my own project, I will abide by my criterion of simplicity and as final apology can only quote Samuel Johnson:

> It is impossible for an expositor not to write too little for some and too much for others. He can only judge what is necessary by his own experience; and how long soever he may deliberate, will at last explain many lines which the learned will think impossible to be mistaken and omit many for which the ignorant will want his help. These are censures merely relative, and must be quietly endured.

The PENDEX is envisioned as a general index, a general working tool for the collector as well as the researcher, and I hope that as such it will be of value.

THE PENDEX

SECTION I

REAL NAMES (RN)

The following is a listing of each author's Real
Name, followed by the pseudonyms used. Collaborative Pen Names (CPN), House Names (HN), and Stratemeyer Syndicate Names (SSN) are identified as such.

AARONS, EDWARD S.: 1916-1975
  Paul Ayers
  E.S. Ronns

ABBOTT, EDWIN A.: 1838-1926
  A. Square

ABRAHAMSEN, CHRISTINE
  Cristabel

ACKERMAN, FORREST J.: b. 1916
  Dr. Acula
  Sylvius Agricola
  S.F. Balboa
  Nick Beal
  Jacques DeForest Erman
  Laurajean Ermayne
  Mirta Forsto: CPN
  Coil Kepac
  Allis Kerlay
  Alden Lorraine
  Katarin Markov Merritt
  Seena Nader
  Astrid Notte
  Forry Rhodan
  Spenser Strong
  Vespertina Torgosi
  Allis Villette
  Claire Voyant
  Hubert George Welles
  Weaver Wright

ADAMS, CLEVE FRANKLIN: 1895-1949
  Franklin Charles
  John Spain

ADAMS, HARRIET STRATEMEYER
  (See Section V, Stratemeyer Syndicate Names.)

ADAMS, HERBERT: 1874-1952
  Jonathan Gray

ADAMS, J.: fl. c. 1903
  Skelton Kuppord

ADAMS, WILLIAM T.: 1822-1897
  Warren T. Ashton
  Irving Brown
  Clingham Hunter, M.D.
  Brooks McCormick
  Old Stager
  Oliver Optic
  Gale Winterton

ALBERT, MARVIN H.
  Nick Quarry
  Anthony Rome

ALLEN, HENRY F.: fl. c. 1891
  Pruning Knife

ALLEN, WILLIAM HENRY: b. 1912
  Clay Fisher
  Will Henry

AMBLER, ERIC: b. 1909
  Eliot Reed: CPN

AMIS, KINGSLEY (William): b. 1922
  Robert Markham

ANDERSON, POUL (William): b. 1926
  Pendleton Book
  A.A. Craig
  Winston P. Sanders

ARMSTRONG, CHARLOTTE: 1905-1969
  Jo Valentine

ARMSTRONG, TERRANCE (Ian Fytton): 1912-1970
  John Gawsworth

ASHTON, WINIFRED: 1888-1965
  Diana Cortis
  Clemence Dane

ASHTON-GWATKIN, FRANK: fl. c. 1929
 John Paris

ASIMOV, ISAAC: b. 1920
 Dr. A
 George E. Dale
 Paul French

ATHANAS, WILLIAM VERNE
 Bill Colson

ATHERTON, GERTRUDE: 1857-1948
 Frank Lin

AUBRAY, FRANK
 Fenton Ash
 Frank Atkins (According to the British Library, Aubray's
  real name was Frank Atkins; this source was first noted
  in *Fantasy Collector's Annual*, 1974 edition. It was also
  documented by Aubray himself through a series of books
  autographed with inscriptions by him, now in the collec-
  tion of Mr. Gerry de la Ree, Saddle River, N.J.)

AUSTIN, MARY: fl. c. 1910
 Gordon Stairs

AVALLONE, MICHAEL: b. 1924
 James Blaine
 Nick Carter: HN
 Troy Conway
 Priscilla Dalton
 Mark Dane
 Jean-Anne De Pre
 Dora Highland
 Steve Michaels
 Dorothea Nile
 Edwina Noone
 Vance Staton
 Sidney Stuart

AYCOCK, ROGER D.: b. 1914
 Roger Dee
 John Starr

BAKER, W. HOWARD
 (See Sexton Blake in Section IV.)

BALDWIN, OLIVER: fl. c. 1924
 Martin Hussingtree

BALLARD, WILLIS TODHUNTER: b. 1903
 Brian Agar
 P.D. Ballard

BALLARD, WILLIS TODHUNTER (cont'd)
W.T. Ballard
Willis T. Ballard
Parker Bonner
Sam Bowie
Hunter D'Allard
Harrison Hunt
John Hunter
Neil MacNeil
John Shepherd

BALLINGER, WILLIAM S.: b. 1912
Bill S. Ballinger
Frederick Freyer
B.X. Sanborn

BALTER, E.
Arthur Cooke: CPN

BALZAC, HONORÉ DE: 1799-1850
Horace de Saint-Aubin

BANGS, JOHN KENDRICK: 1862-1922
Two Wags: CPN

BARBER, MARGARET: 1869-1901
Michael Fairless

BARCLAY, FLORENCE L.: fl. c. 1927
Oliver Sandys

BARCLAY, MARGUERITE F.: fl. c. 1927
Helene Barczynka

BARGONE, CHARLES: 1875-1957
Claud Farrere

BARHAM, RICHARD (Henry): 1788-1845
Thomas Ingoldsby

BARKER, LEONARD N.: fl. c. 1935
L. Noel

BARNARD, MARJORIE FAITH
M. Barnard Eldershaw: CPN

BARNES, ARTHUR K(elvin): 1911-1970
Dave Barnes
Kelvin Kent: HN

BARR, ROBERT: 1850-1912
Luke Sharp

BARRETT, ALFRED W.: fl. c. 1895
R. Andom

BARRIE, SIR JAMES M.: 1860-1937
   Gavin Ogilvy

BARTEL, PHILIP J.
   Philip Barshofsky

BARTON, EUSTACE R.: fl. c. 1907
   Robert Eustace

BARTON, JOHN: 1880-1938
   Johnny Gruelle

BATES, HARRY: b. 1900
   Anthony Gilmore: CPN
   A.R. Holmes
   Quien Sabe (Short stories under this PN are written by Harry
      Bates; novels under this PN are written by Jackson
      Gregory.)
   H.G. Winter: CPN

BAUM, L(yman) FRANK: 1856-1919
   Floyd Akers (Akens?)
   Laura Bancroft
   Capt. Hugh Fitzgerald
   Schuyler Staunton
   Edith Van Dyne
   (*The Laughing Dragon of Oz*, credited to Baum, was actually
      written by his son, Frank J. Baum, some years after Baum's
      death. This was verified through the International Wizard
      of Oz Club in the Autumn 1968 edition of the *Baum Bugle*.)

BAXTER, JOHN
   Martin Loran: CPN

BEARDSLEY, AUBREY (Vincent): 1872-1897
   Philip Broughton
   Giulio Floriani
   Albert Foschter

BECHDOLT, JOHN ERNEST: b. 1884
   Jack Bechdolt

BECK, LILY ADAMS: d. 1931
   E. Barrington
   Louis Moresby

BEDFORD-JONES, H(enry James O'Brien): 1887-1949
   H. Bedford-Jones
   Samri Frikell
   John Wycliffe

BEHONI, SAMUEL
   Atlantis Hallam

BEITH, JOHN HAY: fl. c. 1926
  Ian Hay

BELFOUR, HUGH J.: fl. c. 1821
  St. John Dorset

BELL, ERIC TEMPLE: 1883-1960
  Richard C. Badger
  J.T.
  John Taine
  James Temple

BELL, JOHN KEBLE: fl. c. 1919
  Keble Howard

BENJAMIN, HAROLD R.W.: fl. c. 1939
  J. Abner Peddiwell
  Raymond Wayne

BENNET, GERTRUDE: 1884-1939?
  Francis Stephens

BENNET, ROBERT A.: fl. c. 1913
  Lee Robinet

BENSON, ALLEN INGVALD
  Victor Valding

BERESFORD, LESLIE: fl. c. 1918
  Pan

BESSIERE, RICHARD
  F. Richard-Bessiere: CPN

BESTER, ALFRED: b. 1913
  John Lennox
  Sonny Powell

BICKERSTAFFE-DREW, FRANCIS B.: fl. c. 1858
  John Ayscough

BINDER, EARL (Andreas): b. 1904
  Eando Binder: CPN
  John Coleridge: CPN
  Dean D. O'Brien: CPN

BINDER, OTTO (Oscar): 1911-1974
  Eando Binder: CPN
  John Coleridge: CPN
  Will Garth: HN
  Gordon A. Giles
  Dean D. O'Brien: CPN

BIRKIN, CHARLES LLOYD: b. 1907
  Charles Lloyd

BIRON, HENRY C.: fl. c. 1887
  Hyder Ragged

BIXBY, JEROME: b. 1923
  Jay B. Drexel
  Thornecliff Herrick
  Emerson Jans
  D.B. Lewis
  Harry Neal
  Albert Russell
  J. Russell
  M. St. Vivant

BLAIR, ANDREW J.: fl. c. 1931
  Hamish Blair

BLAIR, ERIC ANDREW: 1903-1950
  George Orwell

BLASSINGAME, WYATT
  William Rainey

BLISH, JAMES (Benjamin): 1921-1975
  William Atheling, Jr.
  Donald Laverty: CPN
  Marcus Lyons
  John Mac Dougal: CPN
  Arthur Merlin
  Luke Torley

BLIXEN, KAREN: 1885-1962
  Pierre Andrezel
  Isak Dinesen

BLOCH, ROBERT: b. 1917
  Tarleton Fiske
  Nathen Hinden
  Collier Young

BLYTH, HARRY: 1852-1898
  Hal Meredith (See Sexton Blake in Section IV.)

BOARDMAN, JOHN
  Roger Herwell

BOEX, H.H.H.: 1856-1940
  J.H. Aine Rosney

BOGART, WILLIAM
  Wallace Brooker: HN
  Russ Hale
  Grant Lane
  Kenneth Robeson: HN

BOND, NELSON S(lade): b. 1908
  George Danzel
  Hubert Mavity

BORDES, FRANÇOIS
  Francis Carsac

BOTT, HENRY
  Charles Recour

BOWEN, ROBERT SIDNEY: 1901-1977
  Lt. Scott Morgan: HN

BOWER, B(ertha) M(uzzy): 1871-1940
  B.M. Sinclair

BOYD, LYLE U.
  Boyd Ellanby: CPN

BOYD, WILLIAM C.
  Boyd Ellanby: CPN

BRADBURY, RAY (Douglas): b. 1920
  D.R. Banat
  Leonard Douglas
  William Elliott
  Leonard Spaulding
  Brett Sterling: HN

BRADLEY, MARIAN ZIMMER: b. 1930
  Brian Morley
  Elfreida Rivers

BRASH, MARGARET M.: fl. c. 1933
  John Kendall

BREBNOR, PERCY: fl. c. 1899
  Christian Lys

BRETNOR, REGINALD C.: b. 1911
  Grendel Briarton

BRIDGES, THOMAS C.: fl. c. 1924
  Christopher Beck

BRIGHT, MARY C(havelita Dunne): fl. c. 1898
  George Egerton

BRINEY, ROBERT EDWARD: b. 1933
  Andrew Duane

BROCKIES, ENID F.: fl. c. 1937
  Countess Helene Magriska

BROOKS, EDWY SEARLES: 1889-1965
  (See Sexton Blake in Section IV.)
  Robert W. Comrade

BROWN, FREDRIC: 1906-1972
  Felix Grahame

BROWN, JOHN MACMILLAN: fl. c. 1903
  Godfrey Sweven

BROWN, ZENITH JONES: b. 1898
  Leslie Ford
  David Frome

BROWNE, HOWARD: b. 1908
  Alexander Blade: HN
  William Brengle: HN
  H.B. Carleton: HN
  Lawrence Chandler: HN
  John Evans: HN
  Lee Francis: HN
  John X. Pollard: HN

BRUCE, KENNETH: fl. c. 1909
  Didrick Crayon, Jr.

BRUECKEL, FRANCIS J.
  Frank J. Bridge

BRULLER, JEAN: b. 1902
  Jean Vercors

BRUNNER, JOHN (Kilian-Houston): b. 1934
  K. Houston Brunner
  John Loxmith
  Trevor Staines
  Keith Woodcott

BUCKNER, MARY DALE
  Donald Dale

BUDRYS, ALGERDAS (Jonas): b. 1931
  Algis Budrys
  Paul Janvier

BULMER, (Henry) KENNETH: b. 1921
  Ernest Corley
  Arthur Frazier: HN
  Adam Hardy
  Kenneth Johns: CPN
  Philip Kent
  Neil Langholm
  Karl Maras
  Nelson Sherwood
  Tully Zetford

BULWER-LYTTON, E(dward Robert): fl. c. 1863
  Owen Meredith

BURKHILDER, EDWIN
  G. Wayman Jones: HN

BURKITT, FREDERICK: fl. c. 1918
  Gregory Saben: CPN

BURKS, ARTHUR J.: 1898-1974
  Estill Critchie
  Burke MacArthur
  Spencer Whitney

BURRAGE, ALFRED MC CLELLAND: b. 1889
  Ex-Private X

BURROUGHS, EDGAR RICE: 1875-1950
  Norman Bean
  John Tyler McCulloch

BURROUGHS, WILLIAM S.: b. 1914
  William Lee

BURTON, ELIZABETH J.: b. 1908
  Susan Alice Kerby

BUTLER, SAMUEL: 1835-1902
  John Pickard Owen
  William Bickersteth Owen
  (Butler used both of these PN's in one book, *The Fair Haven*,
    published in 1873. Under the J.P. Owen PN he wrote the
    book; under the W.B. Owen PN he included a memoir of the
    supposed author.)

BYRNE, STUART JAMES
  John Bloodstone
  Howard Dare
  Marx Kaye

CABELL, JAMES BRANCH: 1879-1958
  Branch Cabell

CAMPBELL, GABRIELLE: fl. c. 1909
  Marjorie Bowen
  Joseph Shearing

CAMPBELL, JOHN W(ood), JR.: 1910-1971
  Karl van Campen
  Arthur McCann
  Don A. Stuart

CAPPS, CARROLL M.: 1917-1971
  C.C. MacApp

CARR, JOHN DICKSON: 1906-1977
  Carr Dickson
  Carter Dickson

CARR, TERRY: b. 1937
  Norman Edwards: CPN

CARTER, JOHN FRANKLIN: 1897–1967
  Jay Franklin

CARTER, JOHN L.J.: fl. c. 1937
  Compton Irving

CARTMELL, ROBERT: fl. c. 1929
  Robert Tarnacre

CARTMILL, CLEVE: 1908–1964
  Michael Corbin

CASELEYR, CAMILLE (Auguste Marie): b. 1909
  Jack Danvers

CASSIDAY, BRUCE: b. 1920
  Carson Bingham
  Max Day

CASWELL, EDWARD A.: fl. c. 1900
  Myself & Another

CAVE, HUGH B.
  Allen Beck
  Geoffrey Vance

CAWTHORN, JIM
  Desmond Reid: HN (See Sexton Blake in Section IV.)

CHADWICK, PAUL: 1902–1972
  Chester Hawks: HN
  Brant House: HN

CHALLANS, MARY: b. 1905
  Mary Renault

CHAMBERS, PHILIP
  Desmond Reid: HN (See Sexton Blake in Section IV.)

CHAMBLISS, JOHN
  (See Nick Carter in Section IV.)

CHAMBLISS, PHILIP
  Desmond Reid: HN (See Sexton Blake in Section IV.)

CHAMPION, D.L.
  G. Wayman Jones: HN

CHANCE, JOHN NEWTON
  John Lymington
  Desmond Reid: HN (See Sexton Blake in Section IV.)

CHANDLER, A. BERTRAM: b. 1912
  Andrew Dunstan
  George Whitley

CHAPMAN, MARGARET STORM: b. 1897
  Storm Jameson

CHAPPELL, GEORGE S.: 1878-1946
  Walter E. Traprock

CHARTERIS, MARY EVELYN: 1887-1960
  Lady Cynthia Asquith

CHIBBETT, H.S.W.
  A. Hastwa

CHRISTIE, AGATHA: 1890-1976
  Mary Westmacott

CLARK, CHARLES BADGER: 1883-1957
  Badger Clark

CLARK, CHARLES H.
  Max Adeler

CLARK, CHARLOTTE M.: b. c. 1878
  Charles M. Clay

CLARK, JOHN D.
  Fletcher Pratt (This PN was due to a publisher's error, as
    Fletcher Pratt is a totally separate author in his own
    right, and so far as is known, Clark never used a PN.
    However, Clark's *Silicone World*, published in *Startling
    Stories*, Dec. 1952, was mistakenly credited to Pratt, and
    the confusion between these two writers still occasionally
    persists.)

CLARK, PHILIP
  (See Nick Carter in Section IV.)

CLARKE, ARTHUR C(harles): b. 1917
  E.G. O'Brien
  Charles Willis

CLARKE, GEORGE S.: fl. c. 1891
  A. Nelson Seaforth

CLAYTON, RICHARD: b. 1907
  William Haggard

CLEMENS, SAMUEL L.: 1835-1910
  Mark Twain

CLERY, WILLIAM: fl. c. 1900
  Austin Fryers

CLINTON, EDWIN M.: b. 1926
  Anthony More

COBBE, FRANCES P.: fl. c. 1877
  Merlin Nostradamus

COCKBURN, CLAUD: b. 1904
  James Helvick

COHEN, CHESTER
  Chester B. Conant

COLES, CYRIL HENRY: 1899–1965
  Manning Coles: CPN
  Francis Gaite: CPN

COLLINS, J.L.: fl. c. 1874
  Jonquil

CONKLIN, (Edward) GROFF: 1904–1968
  W.B. de Graeff

CONNELL, ALLAN
  Alan Conn

CONNOLLY, CYRIL (Vernon): b. 1903
  Palinurus
  Vercors

COOK, WILLIAM WALLACE: 1867–1933
  (See Nick Carter in Section IV.)
  John Milton Edwards
  W.B. Lawson

COOKE, MRS. LEONARD: fl. c. 1921
  Joan Conquest

COOKE, MILLEN
  Alexander Blade: HN

COOPER, EDMUND: b. 1926
  Richard Avery

COPPEL, ALFRED: b. 1921
  Sol Galaxan
  Robert Cham Gilman
  Derfla Leppoc

CORY, MATILDA W.: fl. c. 1904
  M.W.M. Cory
  Winifred Grahame

CORY, VIVIAN: fl. c. 1924
  Victoria Cross

CORYELL, JOHN RUSSELL: 1848–1924
  (See Nick Carter in Section IV.)
  Nick Carter: HN
  Bertha M. Clay: HN
  Tyman Currio: HN
  Lillian R. Drayton: HN
  Julia Edwards: HN
  Geraldine Fleming: HN

CORYELL, JOHN RUSSELL (cont'd)
  Margaret Grant: HN
  Barbara Howard: HN
  Harry DuBois Milman: HN
  Milton Quarterman: HN
  Lucy May Russell: HN

COULSON, JUANITA: b. 1933
  John Jay Wells

COULSON, ROBERT
  Thomas Stratton: CPN

COUNSELMAN, MARY ELIZABETH: b. 1911
  Eli Colter

COVE, JOSEPH WALTER: b. 1891
  Lewis Gibbs

COX, ANTHONY BERKELEY
  Anthony Berkeley
  Francis Iles

COX, ARTHUR JEAN
  Ralph Carghill
  Jean Cox

COXE, EDWARD D.: fl. c. 1885
  A Fugitive

CREASEY, JOHN: 1908-1973
  Gordon Ashe
  M.E. Cooke
  Norman Deane
  Robert Caine Frazer
  Patrick Gill
  Michael Halliday
  Charles Hogarth
  Brian Hope
  Colin Hughes
  Kyle Hunt
  Abel Mann
  Peter Manton
  J.J. Marric
  Richard Martin
  Anthony Moreton
  Ken Ranger
  William K. Reilly
  Tex Riley
  Jeremy York

CRELLIN, H.N.: fl. c. 1888
  Al Arawiyah

CRICHTON, J. MICHAEL: b. 1942
  Jeffrey Hudson
  John Lange

CROFT-COOKE, RUPERT: b. 1903
  Leo Bruce
  Taylor Croft

CRONIN, BERNARD: b. 1884
  Dennis Adair
  Eric North

CROSBY, HARRY C.
  Christopher Anvil

CROSS, JOHN KEIR: 1914-1967
  Stephen McFarland

CROSSEN, KENDALL (Foster): b. 1910
  Bennett Barclay
  M.E. Chaber
  Ken Crossen
  Richard Foster
  Christopher Monig
  Clay Richards

CUMMINGS, RAY: 1887-1957
  John W. Campbell, Jr. (This was a publisher's error.
  Brigands of the Moon was a well-known space opera by
  Cummings; during the 1930's, John W. Campbell, Jr. wrote
  a number of similar space operas. When the Duchess Edi-
  tion [Canadian, undated] of *Brigands* was published,
  through error it was credited to Campbell, rather than
  Cummings. Full documentation of this error is in Donald
  Tuck's *Encyclopedia*.)
  Ray King
  Ray P. Shotwell
  Gabriel Wilson

CURRY, TOM
  Jackson Cole: HN

CURZON-HERRICK, KATHLEEN H.: fl. c. 1935
  Maud Cairnes

DANIEL, GLYN (Edmund): b. 1914
  Dilwyn Rees

DANNAY, FREDERIC: b. 1905
  Daniel Nathan: PN
  Ellery Queen: CPN
  Barnaby Ross: CPN

DANNENBERG, NORMAN
  (Through an editor's error, N. Dannenberg was employed as
    N. Daniels and N. Danberg, and never bothered to rectify
    the mistake. This is verified in *Duende* 2.)
  John Benton: HN
  Wallace Brooker: HN
  Norman Danberg
  Norman Daniels
  G. Wayman Jones: HN
  Lt. Scott Morgan: HN
  Kenneth Robeson: HN
  Robert Wallace: HN

D'APERY, HELEN: fl. c. 1903
  Olive Harper

D'ARCY, JACK
  G. Wayman Jones: HN

DAVIES, HOWELL
  Andrew Marvell

DAVIS, FREDERICK CLYDE: b. 1902
  Murdo Coombs
  Stephen Ransome
  Curtis Steele: HN

DAVIS, FREDERICK W.: 1853-1933
  (See Nick Carter in Section IV.)

DAVIS, HAROLD A.: 1902-1955
  Kenneth Robeson: HN

DAVIS, JAMES: 1853-1907
  Owen Hall

DAY-LEWIS, CECIL: 1904-1972
  Nicholas Blake

De BANZIE, ERIC: fl. c. 1928
  Gregory Baxter: CPN

De BURY, F. BLAZE: fl. c. 1904
  F. Dickberry

De CAMP, L(yon) SPRAGUE: b. 1907
  Lyman R. Lyon
  J. Wentworth Wells

DEEPING, GEORGE WARWICK: 1877-1950
  Warwick Deeping
  George Warwick

DEER, M. JANE
  M.J. Deer: CPN

De FOIGNY, GABRIEL: fl. c. 1693
  James Sadeur

De KREMER, RAYMOND: 1887-1964
  John Flanders
  Jean Ray

de la MARE, WALTER: 1873-1956
  Walter Ramal

del REY, LESTER: b. 1915
  (See also Paul W. Fairman, Section I.)
  John Alvarez
  Cameron Hall
  Marion Henry
  Philip James
  Wade Kaempfert
  Edson McCann
  Philip St. John
  Charles Satterfield: HN
  Erik Van Lhin

De MATTOS, MRS.: fl. c. 1892
  T. Hertz-Garden

De MELIKOFF, JODI
  Jody McCarter: CPN

DENNIS, WALTER
  Dennis McDermott: CPN

DENT, LESTER: 1904-1959
  John Blaine: SSN
  Harmon Cash
  Maxwell Grant: HN
  Kenneth Roberts: HN
  Kenneth Robeson: HN
  Tim Ryan

De PATOT, SIMON TYSSOT: b. c. 1743
  James Massey

DERLETH, AUGUST: 1909-1971
  Stephen Grendon
  Tally Mason
  Michael West

D'ESMENARD, JEAN: fl. c. 1924
  Jean D'Esme

De WEASE, GENE
  Thomas Stratton: CPN

De WEINDECK, WINTELER, U.M.C.: fl. c. 1889
  George Z. Fighton

DEY, F. VAN RENSSELAER: 1861-1922
  (See Nick Carter in Section IV.)

DICK, KAY: b. 1915
  Jeremy Scott

DIKTY, MAY
  Julain Chain

DILLON, DORA A.: fl. c. 1924
  Patricia Wentworth

DINGLE, AYLWARD E.: fl. c. 1947
  Sinbad

DISCH, THOMAS: b. 1940
  Thom Demijohn: CPN
  Dobbin Thorp

DITZEN, RUDOLF: fl. c. 1937
  Hans Fallada

DIVINE, ARTHUR DURHAM: b. 1904
  David Divine (This is a legitimate PN; however, there is
    also a mystery writer whose real name is David M. Divine.)
  David Rame

DIVINE, DAVID MACDONALD: b. 1920
  (See Arthur Durham Divine, Section I.)
  Dominick Divine

DOCKWEILER, HARRY
  Paul Dennis LaVond: CPN
  Dirk Wylie

DODGSON, CHARLES L(utwidge): 1832-1898
  Lewis Carroll

DOLGOV, BORIS
  Dolbokov: CPN

DONALDSON, DALE C.: 1922-1977
  William Chamberlain

DONNELLY, IGNATIUS: 1831-1901
  Edmund Boisgilbert

DONOVAN, LAURENCE: d. 1957?
  Wallace Brooker: HN
  Clifford Goodrich: HN
  Austin Gridley: HN
  Kenneth Robeson: HN

DOROSCHENKO, LEO
  Faith Lincoln: CPN

Real Names   21

DOUGLAS, MYRTLE R.
  Mirta Forsto: CPN
  Morojo

DOUGLAS, NORMAN: fl. c. 1901
  Normyx

DOWNEY, EDMUND: fl. c. 1890
  F.M. Allen

DRAGO, HENRY SINCLAIR: b. 1888
  Stewart Cross
  Kirk Deming
  Will Ermine
  Bliss Lomax
  J. Wesley Putnam
  Grant Sinclair

DRESSER, DAVIS: 1904-1977
  Asa Baker
  Matthew Blood
  Kathryn Culver
  Don Davis
  Hal Debrett
  Brett Halliday
  Anthony Scott
  Peter Shelley
  Anderson Wayne

DRIANT, EMILE A.: fl. c. 1910
  Captain Danrit

Du BOIS, EDWARD: b. c. 1800
  Count Reginald de St. Leon

DUNKERLEY, WILLIAM A.: fl. c. 1924
  John Oxenham

ECCLES, CHARLOTTE O.: fl. c. 1897
  Hal Godfrey

EDEN, DOROTHY
  Mary Paradise

EDWARDS, FREDERICK A.: fl. c. 1936
  Charman Edwards

ELDERSHAW, FLORA (Sydney Patricia)
  M. Barnard Eldershaw: CPN

ELIOT, GEORGE FIELDING
  C.K.M. Scanlon: HN

ELLIK, RONALD D.: 1938-1968
  Frederick Davies: HN

ELLIOT, BRUCE
  Maxwell Grant: HN
  (Elliott also wrote Nick Carter novelettes that appeared in
    The Shadow magazine under his own name. See Nick Carter,
    Section IV.)

ELLISON, HARLAN; b. 1934
  Lee Archer: HN
  Cortwainer Bird
  Ellis Hart

ELVSTAD, SVEN: 1864-1934
  Stein Riverton

ELY, GEORGE: fl. c. 1911
  Herbert Strang: CPN

EMMANUEL, VICTOR ROUSSEAU: 1879-1960
  H.M. Egbert
  Victor Rousseau
  Clyve Trent

EMSHWILLER, EDMUND (Alexander): b. 1925
  Emsh
  Ed Emsh

EPSTEIN, SAMUEL
  (See Section V, Stratemeyer Syndicate Names.)

ERNST, PAUL: b. 1902
  George Alden Edson
  Kenneth Robeson: HN
  Paul Frederick Stern

ERNSTING, WALTER: b. 1920
  Clark Darlton
  F. MacPatterson

EVANS, E. EVERETT: 1893-1958
  Harry J. Gardener
  H.E. Verett

EVANS, MRS. E. EVERETT (Thelma Evans?)
  Hamm Edwards
  T.D. Hamm

EVANS, GEORGE
  Brandon Bird: CPN

EVANS, KAY
  Brandon Bird: CPN

EVELYN, JOHN MICHAEL
  Michael Underwood

EVERETT, MRS. H.D.: fl. c. 1905
  Theo Douglas

FAIRBANKS, CHARLES BULLARD: 1827-1859
  Aguecheek

FAIRMAN, PAUL W.: 1916-1977
  Adam Chase: HN
  Lester del Rey (del Rey supplied the outlines for 5 juvenile
    books; these were all written by Fairman, but published by
    Scholastic Books under del Rey's name.)
  Clee Garson: HN
  E.K. Jarvis: HN
  Ivar Jorgensen: HN
  Ellery Queen, Jr. (Fairman used the Queen PN for one book
    only, *A Study in Terror*. See *Locus* 206.)

FANTHORPE, ROBERT LIONEL: b. 1935
  Erle Barton
  Leo Brett
  Bron Fane
  John E. Muller: HN
  Lionel Roberts
  Trebor Thorpe
  Pel Torro
  Karl Ziegfried: HN

FARGUS, FREDERICK JOHN: 1847-1885
  Hugh Conway

FARJEON, JOSEPH JEFFERSON: 1883-1955
  Anthony Swift

FARLIE, GERARD T.
  Sapper (See also H.C. McNeile, Section I.)

FARMER, PHILIP JOSÉ: b. 1918
  William Norfolk
  Kilgore Trout

FARNESE, A.: fl. c. 1896
  Franchezzo

FAST, HOWARD (Melvin): b. 1914
  E.V. Cunningham
  Walter Erickson

FAUST, FREDERICK: 1892-1944
  Frank Austin
  George Owen Baxter
  Lee Bolt
  Max Brand
  Walter G. Butler

FAUST, FREDERICK (cont'd)
  George Challis
  Martin Dexter
  Evin Evan
  Evan Evans
  John Frederick
  Frederick Frost
  Dennis Lawton
  David Manning
  Peter Henry Moreland
  Hugh Owen
  Arthur Preston
  Nicholas Silver
  Henry Uriel

FAWCETT, FRANK D.: fl. c. 1935
  Simpson Stokes

FEARN, JOHN RUSSELL: 1908-1960
  Geoffrey Armstrong
  Thornton Ayre
  Hugo Blayn
  Morton Boyce
  Dennis Clive
  John Cotten
  Polton Cross
  Astron Del Martia
  Mark Denholm
  Douglas Dodd
  Sheridan Drew
  Max Elston
  Wesley Firth
  Volsted Gridban: HN
  Malcolm Hartley
  C.G. Holt
  Conrad Holt
  Frank Jones
  Marvin Kayne
  King Lang (See also E.C. Tubb, Section I.)
  Herbert Lloyd
  Paul Lorraine
  Victor Magroon
  Dom Passante
  Francis Rose
  Laurence Rose
  L.F. Ross
  Ward Ross
  Joan Saegar
  Bryan Shaw

John Slate
Vargo Statten
K. Thomas
Earl Titan
Arthur Waterhouse
Ephraim Winiki

FELDMAN, A(natole) F(rance)
  G. Wayman Jones: HN

FIGGIS, DARRELL: fl. c. 1923
  Michael Ireland

FIRTH, VIOLET MARY: 1890-1946
  Dion Fortune

FISCHER, BRUNO: b. 1908
  Russell Gray
  Harrison Storm

FISH, ROBERT L.: b. 1912
  Robert L. Eire
  Robert L. Pike

FISHER, STEPHEN GOULD: b. 1912
  Stephen Gould
  Grant Lane

FITZPATRICK, ERNEST H.: fl. c. 1895
  Hugo Barnaby

FLACK, ISAAC H.: fl. c. 1937
  Harvey Graham

FLAMMARION, (Nicolas) CAMILLE: 1842-1925
  Camille Flammarion

FLEMING-ROBERTS, G.T.
  George Chance: HN
  Brant House: HN
  G. Wayman Jones: HN
  Robert Wallace: HN

FOOT, MICHAEL: fl. c. 1943
  Cassius

FORD, COREY: b. 1902
  John Riddell

FOSTER, GEORGE C(ecil): fl. c. 1939
  Seaforth

FOSTER, W. BERT: 1869-1929
  (See Nick Carter in Section IV.)

FOWLER, FRANK
  Borden Chase

FOWLER, KENNETH
  Clark Brooker

FOX, GARDNER F.: b. 1911
  Jefferson Cooper
  Paul Dean (comics)
  James Kendricks
  Simon Majors
  Kevin Matthews
  Clement Purvis
  Bart Somers

FRANKAU, MRS. JULIA: fl. c. 1916
  Frank Danby

FREEMAN, KATHLEEN: b. 1897
  Mary Fitt

FREEMAN, RICHARD AUSTIN: 1862-1943
  Clifford Ashdown: CPN
  R. Austin Freeman

FRENCH, ALICE: 1850-1934
  Octave Thanet

FREYBE, HEIDI HUBERTA: b. 1912
  Martha Albrand
  Katrin Holland
  Christine Lambert

FRIEND, OSCAR J.: 1897-1963
  Owen Fox Jerome
  Ford Smith

FYFE, HORACE B.: b. 1918
  Andrew MacDuff

GABRIELSON, ERNEST (Lewis)
  Anthony Cotrion
  John Gabriel

GALLUN, RAYMOND Z(inke): b. 1910
  Arthur Allport
  William Callahan
  Don Elstar
  E.V. Raymond

GALPIN, ALFRED
  Consul Hastings (This PN was also attributed, incorrectly,
    to H.P. Lovecraft.)

GANLEY, W. PAUL
  Toby Duane

GARDNER, ERLE STANLEY: 1889-1970
  Kyle Corning
  A.A. Fair
  Charles M. Green
  Carleton Kendrake
  Charles J. Kenny
  Robert Parr
  Les Tillray

GARIS, HOWARD
  Victor Appleton: SSN

GARRETT, RANDALL (Phillips)
  Gordon Aghill: HN
  Grandall Barreton
  Alexander Blade: HN
  Ralph Burke: HN
  David Gordon
  Richard Greer: HN
  Ivar Jorgensen: HN
  Darrel T. Langart
  Clyde Mitchell: HN
  Mark Phillips: CPN
  Robert Randall: CPN
  Leonard G. Spencer: HN
  S.M. Tenneshaw: HN
  Gerold Vance: HN

GARTON, DURHAM KEITH
  Durham Keyes
  Al Ryan

GEIER, CHESTER S.: b. 1921
  Guy Archett
  Alexander Blade: HN
  P.F. Costello: HN
  Waren Kastel: HN
  S.M. Tenneshaw: HN
  Gerold Vance: HN
  Peter Worth: HN

GEISEL, THEODORE (Seuss): b. 1904
  Theo LeSieg
  Dr. Seuss

GEORGE, PETER: 1924-1966
  Peter Bryant

GERMANO, PETER B.
  Barry Cord

GERNSBACK, HUGO: 1884-1967
  Greno Gashback
  Gus N. Habergook
  Grego Vanshuck

GERVEE, BARONTE: fl. c. 1935
  Gerve Baronte

GIBSON, JOE
  John Bridger
  Carlton Furth

GIBSON, WALTER D.: b. 1897
  Harry Charlot
  Maxwell Grant: HN

GILLINGS, WALTER L.: b. 1911
  Thomas Sheridan

GLEMSER, BERNARD: b. 1908
  Robert Crane

GLIDDEN, FREDERICK DILLEY: 1908-1975
  Luke Short

GLIDDEN, JONATHAN H.: 1907-1957
  Peter Dawson

GLUT, DONALD FRANK: b. 1944
  Don Grant
  Johnny Jason
  Victor Morrison
  Rod Richmond
  Mick Rogers
  Dr. Spektor
  Dale Steele
  Bradley D. Thorne

GOLD, H(orace) L.: b. 1914
  Clyde Crain Campbell
  Dudley Dell
  Harold C. Fosse

GOMPERTZ, MARTIN L.: 1886-1951
  Ganpat

GOODCHILD, GEORGE: b. 1888
  Alan Dare

GOODE, ARTHUR RUSSELL
  Arthur Russell

GOODWIN, HAROLD
  John Blaine: SSN

GOTTFRIED, THEODORE (Mark): b. 1928
  Leslie Behan
  Harry Gregory
  Ted Mark
  Katharine Tobias

GOULART, RON(ald Joseph): b. 1913
  Josephine Kains
  Kenneth Robeson: HN

GOWING, SIDNEY F.: fl. c. 1920
  John Goodwin

GRAHAM, ROGER (Phillips): 1909–1965
  Clinton Ames
  Robert Arnett: HN
  Franklin Bahl: HN
  Alexander Blade: HN
  Craig Browning
  P.F. Costello: HN
  Sanandana Kumara
  Charles Lee: HN
  Inez McGowan
  Milton Mann: HN
  Rog Phillips
  Melva Rogers
  Chester Rupert
  William Carter Sawtelle: HN
  A.R. Steber: HN
  Gerold Vance: HN
  John Wiley
  Peter Worth: HN

GRAINGER, FRANCIS E.: fl. c. 1903
  Headon Hill

GRAUTOFF, FERDINAND (Heinrich)
  Parabellum

GRAVES, CLOTILDE (Inez Mary): 1863–1932
  Richard Dehan

GRAVES, ROBERT (von Ranke): b. 1895
  John Doyle
  Tom Fool
  FUZE

GRAVES, ROBERT (cont'd)
  B.K. Mallik
  Peccavi
  Barbara Rich: CPN
  Z

GREBANIER, FRANCESCA VINCIGUERRA: b. 1900
  Frances Winwar

GREENER, WILLIAM O.: fl. c. 1895
  Wirt Gerrare

GREENWOOD, JULIA: fl. c. 1944
  Francis Askham

GREGORY, JACKSON: 1882-1943
  Quien Sabe (Short stories by Quien Sabe are written by Harry
    Bates; novels by Quien Sabe are written by Jackson Gregory.)

GREGORY, ORMOND
  W. Wayne Robbins

GRIGSBY, ALCANOAN O.: fl. c. 1900
  Jack Adams

GROSSMAN, JOSEPHINE JUDITH: b. 1923
  Ernest Hamilton
  Cyril Judd: CPN
  Judith Merrill
  Rose Sharon
  Eric Thorstein

GROUSSET, PASCHAL
  S. Laurie

GRUBER, FRANK: 1904-1969
  Stephen Acre
  Charles K. Boston
  Tom Gunn: HN
  C.K.M. Scanlon: HN
  John K. Vedder

GUEZENEC, ALFRED: fl. c. 1883
  Alfred Brehot

GUIN, WYMAN (Woods): b. 1915
  Norman Manasco
  Guy Thorne

GULL, CYRIL A. RANGER
  Guy Thorne

GUNN, JAMES E(dwin): b. 1923
  James A. Gunn
  Edwin James

GUTHRIE, THOMAS A.: 1856-1934
  F. Anstey

GUY, L.: fl. c. 1909
  A Patriot

HAGGARD, J. HARVEY: b. 1913
  The Planet Prince

HALE, MARICE R.: fl. c. 1931
  Maryse Rutledge

HALL, DESMOND
  Anthony Gilmore: CPN
  H.G. Winter: CPN

HAMILTON, EDMUND: 1904-1977
  Alexander Blade: HN
  Robert Castle
  Hugh Davidson
  Will Garth: HN
  Brett Sterling: HN
  S.M. Tenneshaw: HN
  Robert Wentworth

HAMON, LOUIS
  Cheiro

HANKINSON, CHARLES J.: fl. c. 1898
  Clive Holland

HANSHEW, THOMAS W.: 1857-1914
  (See Nick Carter in Section IV.)

HARBAUGH, THOMAS C.: 1849-1924
  (See Nick Carter in Section IV.)

HARDINGE, REX
  (See Sexton Blake in Section IV.)

HARKINS, PETER J.
  John Blaine: SSN

HARKNETT, TERRY
  William M. James: HN
  Charles R. Pike: HN

HARLAND, HENRY: 1861-1905
  Sidney Luska

HARRIS, JOHN BEYNON: 1903-1969
  John Beynon
  Wyndham Parkes
  John Wyndham

HARRIS, LARRY M.: b. 1933
  Laurence M. Janifer (This became his legal name.)
  William Logan
  Mark Phillips: CPN

HARRISON, MARY S.: fl. c. 1896
  Lucas Malet

HARTING, PETER: fl. c. 1871
  Dr. Dioscorides

HARTMANN, FRANZ: fl. c. 1887
  A Student of Occultism

HARVEY, JOHN
  L.J. Coburn: HN
  J.B. Dancer: HN
  John J. McLaglen: HN

HATCH, DAVID P(atterson): fl. c. 1899
  Paul Karishka

HATHWAY, ALAN: 1906-1977
  Clifford Goodrich: HN
  Kenneth Robeson: HN

HAUSER, HEINRICH: b. 1901
  Alexander Blade: HN

HAWKER, MARY E.: fl. c. 1891
  Lance Falconer

HAWKINS, A(nthony) H(ope): 1863-1933
  Anthony Hope

HEALD, LES
  Charnock Walsby

HEARD, H(enry) F(itzgerald): 1889-1971
  Gerald Heard
  H.F. Heard

HEARN, MARY: fl. c. 1892
  Marianne Farningham

HEINLEIN, ROBERT A(nson): b. 1907
  Anson MacDonald
  Lyle Monroe
  John Riverside
  Caleb Saunders
  Simon Yorke

HEMMING, JOHN W.: 1900-1953
  Paul deWreder

HENDERSON, T.
  (See Nick Carter in Section IV.)

HENHAM, ERNEST: fl. c. 1911
  John Trevena

HERNHUTER, ALBERT
  Burt Ahearne

HERON-ALLEN, EDWARD: 1861-1943
  Christopher Blayre

HERSEY, HAROLD: 1892-1956
  Carl Buxton
  Philip Kennedy
  Charles Kiproy
  Larrovitch
  Roy LeMoyne
  Albert Owen
  Arnold Tyson
  Vail Vernon

HETTINGER, JOHN: fl. c. 1931
  Johnhett

HIBBERT, ELEANOR (Burford): b. 1906
  Eleanor Burford
  Philippa Carr
  Elbur Ford
  Victoria Holt
  Kathleen Kellow
  Jean Plaidy
  Ellalice Tate

HIRD, JAMES D(ennis): fl. c. 1894
  Lord Bottsford

HOADLEY, H.O.
  Gene Mitchell

HOAR, ROGER SHERMAN: 1887-1963
  Ralph Milne Farley
  Bennington Orth
  Lt. John Pease
  General X

HOCH, EDWARD D.: b. 1930
  Irwin Booth
  Stephen Dentinger
  Pat McMahon
  R.L. Stephens
  Mister X

HODDER-WILLIAMS, CHRISTOPHER: b. 1926
  James Brogan

HOGG, JAMES: 1770-1835
  The Ettrick Shepherd

HOLDAWAY, NEVILLE (Aldridge): b. 1894
  N.A. Temple-Ellis

HOLDING, JAMES (Clark Carlisle), JR.: b. 1907
  Clark Carlisle
  Ellery Queen, Jr.

HOLDSTOCK, ROB
  Richard Kirk: HN

HOLLY, JOAN C.: b. 1932
  J. Hunter Holly

HOOD, ARCHER: fl. c. 1924
  William Leslie: CPN

HOOKE, CHARLES: fl. c. 1889
  Howard Fielding

HOOKER, FANNY: fl. c. 1869
  Erniest Hoven

HORLER, SYDNEY: 1888-1954
  Peter Cavendish
  Martin Heritage

HORNIG, CHARLES D.: b. 1916
  Derwin Lesser

HOUGH, STANLEY BENNETT: b. 1917
  Rex Gordon
  Bennett Stanley

HOWARD, ALBERT W(aldo): fl. c. 1898
  M. Auburre Hovorre

HOWARD, ROBERT E(rvin): 1906-1936
  Patrick Ervin
  Patrick Howard
  John Taverel
  Sam Walser

HUBBARD, L. RON: b. 1911
  Elron
  Tom Esterbrook
  Michael Keith
  Rene Lafayette
  Legionnaire 14830
  Ken Martin
  John Seabrook
  Kurt VonRachen

HUNGERFORD, MARGARET (Wolfe): 1855-1897
  The Duchess

HUNTER, BLUEBELL M.: fl. c. 1935
  George Lancing

HUNTINGTON, EDWARD S.: fl. c. 1892
  Edward Stanton

HUTCHINSON, ROBERT H.: fl. c. 1934
  Robert Hare

HYLAND, M.E.F.: fl. c. 1901
  Kythe Wylwynne

HYNAM, JOHN (Charles): 1915-1974
  John Kippax

HYND, LAVINIA: fl. c. 1927
  Lavinia Leitch

JAKES, JOHN (William): b. 1932
  Jay Scotland

JAMES, FRANCIS
  James A. Goldthwaite

JAMES, LAURENCE
  L.J. Coburn: HN
  Arthur Frazier: HN
  Charles C. Garrett: HN
  William M. James: HN
  Neil Langholm: HN
  John J. McLaglen: HN
  Jonathan May
  Klaus Netzen
  Christopher Nolan

JAMESON, ANNIE E.: fl. c. 1920
  J.E. Buckrose

JAMESON, MALCOM: 1891-1945
  Colin Keith
  Mary MacGregor

JANIFER, LAURENCE M.: b. 1933
  (See Larry M. Harris, Section I.)

JARDINE, JACK (Owen): b. 1931
  Howard Corey
  Larry Maddock

JENKINS, WILLIAM F(itzgerald): 1896-1975
  William Fitzgerald
  Murray Leinster

JENKS, GEORGE C.: 1850-1929
  (See Nick Carter in Section IV.)

JOHNSON, WALTER RYERSON
  Kenneth Robeson: HN
  Robert Wallace: HN

JOHNSTONE, CHARLES
  An Adept

JONES, ADRIENNE
  Gregory Mason: CPN

JONES, RAYMOND F.: b. 1915
  David Anderson

JONES, VERNON
  Raymond A. Young

JOQUEL, ARTHUR LOUIS, II
  William Graham

JOSCELYN, ARCHIE L.: b. 1889
  A.A. Archer
  Al Cody
  Tex Holt
  Evelyn McKenna
  Lynn Westland

JUDSON, E.Z.C.: 1821-1886
  Ned Buntline

KAHLERT, KARL F.: fl. c. 1794
  Lorenz Flammenburg

KALER, OTIS (James): fl. c. 1893
  James Otis

KARIG, WALTER: 1898-1956
  Julia K. Duncan: SSN
  James Cody Ferris: SSN
  Carolyn Keene: SSN
  Keats Patrick

KAYSER, RONAL
  Dale Clark
  George E. Clark

KELLENBERGER, L.C.: fl. c. 1929
  Henry James

KELLER, DAVID H.: 1880-1967
  Henry Cecil
  Amy Worth

KING, C(harles) DALY: 1895-1963
  Jeremiah Phelan

KIRWAN, THOMAS: fl. c. 1909
  William Wonder

KLASS, PHILIP: b. 1920
  William Tenn

KLEINER, RHEINHART
  Randolph St. John (This PN was also attributed, incorrectly,
    to H.P. Lovecraft.)

KNAUSS, ROBERT: fl. c. 1932
  Major Von Helders

KNIGHT, DAMON F(rancis): b. 1922
  Ritter Conway
  Stuart Fleming
  Donald Laverty: CPN

KNIGHT, K.N.
  Alan Amos
  Stuart Fleming

KNOWLES, MABEL W.: fl. c. 1912
  Lester Lurgan

KORNBLUTH, CYRIL M.: 1923-1958
  Arthur Cooke: CPN
  Cecil Corwin
  Walter C. Davies
  Kenneth Falconer
  S.D. Gottesman: CPN
  Cyril Judd: CPN
  Paul Dennis LaVond: CPN
  Scott Mariner
  Jordan Park: CPN
  Ivor Towers: HN
  Dirk Wiley

KOUYOUMDJIAN, DIKRAN: 1895-1956
  Michael Arlen

KREPPS, ROBERT W(ilson): b. 1919
  Geoff St. Reynard

KRUSE, JUNE (Millichamp): b. 1932
  Karen Anderson

KUBILIUS, WALTER
  K.S. Klimaris

KUMMER, FREDERICK ARNOLD: 1873-1943
  John Arnold
  Arnold Fredericks
  Martin Vaeth

KURNITZ, HARRY
  Marco Page

KUTTNER, HENRY: 1914-1958
  Paul Edmunds
  Noel Gardner
  Will Garth: HN
  James Hall
  Keith Hammond: CPN
  Hudson Hastings: CPN
  Peter Horn: HN
  Kelvin Kent: HN
  Robert O. Kenyon
  C.H. Liddell: CPN
  K.H. Maepen
  Scott Morgan
  Lawrence O'Donnell: CPN
  Lewis Padgett: CPN
  Woodrow Wilson Smith
  Charles Stoddard: HN
  Edward J. Vellin

LAMBERT, LESLIE H.: fl. c. 1928
  A.J. Alan

LAMBURN, RICHMAL C.: fl. c. 1926
  Richmal Crompton

L'AMOUR, LOUIS
  Tex Burns: HN
  Jim Mayo

LANCASTER, WILLIAM J.C.: fl. c. 1926
  Harry Collingwood

LANDA, GERTRUDE
  Aunt Naomi

LANDON, MELVILLE D.: fl. c. 1872
  Eli Perkins

LANE, MARY E.: fl. c. 1890
  Vera Zarovitch

LANGE, JOHN FREDERICK: b. 1931
  John Norman

La SPINA, GREYA: 1880-1969
  Isra Putnam

LAWRENCE, T(homas) E(dward): 1888-1935
  Aircraftsman Ross
  T.E. Shaw

LAYTON, FRANK GEORGE: fl. c. 1909
  Stephen Andrew

LEE, ARTHUR S.G.: fl. c. 1947
  Arthur Lee Gould

LEE, HENRY B.: fl. c. 1872
  Theophilus McCrib

LEE, MANFRED (Bennington): 1905-1971
  Ellery Queen: CPN
  Barnaby Ross: CPN

LEFFINGWELL, ALBERT: fl. c. 1943
  Dana Chambers

LEGER, RAYMOND A.
  Raymond McDonald: CPN

LEIPIAR, LOUISE
  L. Major Reynolds

LEISK, DAVID (Johnson): 1906-1975
  Crockett Johnson

LESLIE, A.
  Jackson Cole: HN
  Bradford Scott

LESLIE, JOSEPHINE A.: fl. c. 1945
  R.A. Dick

LESLIE, MARY ISABEL: fl. c. 1928
  Temple Lane

LESSER, MILTON: b. 1928
  Adam Chase: HN
  Stephen Marlowe
  S.M. Tenneshaw: HN
  C.H. Thames

L'ESTRANGE, C.J.: fl. c. 1911
  Herbert Strang: CPN

LEWIS, ALETHEA: fl. c. 1805
  Eugenia De Acton

LEWIS, BARON Von LUDWIG
  Lewis Holberg

LEWIS, C(live) S(taples): 1898-1963
  Clive Hamilton
  "N.W."
  Nat Whilk

LEWIS, JACK: fl. c. 1935
  (See Sexton Blake in Section IV.)

LEWIS, MARY (Christina): b. 1907
  Christina Brand
  China Thompson

LEY, (Robert) ARTHUR: 1921-1968
  Arthur Sellings

LEY, WILLY: 1906-1969
  John Brown
  Robert Willey

LIN, LESLIE C.B.: b. 1907
  Leslie Charteris
  Bruce Taylor (This PN was used for radio scripts.)

LINEBARGER, PAUL (Myron Anthony): 1913-1966
  Anthony Beardon
  Felix C. Forrest
  Carmichael Smith
  Cordwainer Smith

LIVINGSTON, BERKLEY: b. 1908
  Alexander Blade: HN
  Morris J. Steele: HN

LIVINGSTON, HERB(ert): b. 1916
  Alexander Blade: HN
  H.B. Hickey

LOBO, GEORGE E.: fl. c. 1929
  Oliver Sherry

LOCKE, ROBERT (Donald)
  Roger Arcot

LOMBINO, S.A.: b. 1926
  Curt Cannon
  Hunt Collins
  Evan Hunter
  Ed McBain
  Richard Marsten

LONG, AMELIA REYNOLDS: b. 1904
  Kathleen Buddington Cox: CPN
  Patrick Laing
  Adrian Reynolds
  Peter Reynolds
  Mordred Weir

LONG, FRANK BELKNAP: b. 1903
  Leslie Northen

LOOMIS, NOEL MILLER: 1905-1969
  Sam Allison
  Benj. Miller
  Frank Miller
  Silas Water

LOVECRAFT, H(oward) P(hillips): 1890-1937
  Lawrence Appleton
  Isaac Bickerstaff, Jr.
  John J. Jones
  Humphrey Littlewit
  Archibald Maynwaring
  Henry Paget-Lowe
  Ward Phillips
  Richard Raleigh
  Ames Dorrance Rersley (Rowley)
  Edward Softly
  Augustus T. Swift
  Lewis Theobald, Jr.
  Albert Frederick Willie
  Zoilus

LOWDER, CHRISTOPHER
  (See Sexton Blake in Section IV.)

LOWNDES, ROBERT W.: b. 1916
  Arthur Cooke: CPN
  S.D. Gottesman: CPN
  Mallory Kent
  Paul Dennis LaVond: CPN
  John MacDougal: CPN
  Wilfred Owen Morley
  Richard Morrison
  Carol Rey
  Lawrence Woods: CPN (The Woods PN was also used separately
    by Don Wollheim.)

LUMLEY, BENJAMIN: fl. c. 1843
  Hermes

LUNN, HUGH K.: fl. c. 1924
  Hugh Kingsmill

LUNNEY, FRANK
  Faith Lincoln: CPN

LYNCH, JANE: b. 1941
  Jane Gaskell

LYNDS, DENNIS
  William Arden
  Michael Collins

LYNDS, DENNIS (cont'd)
  Maxwell Grant: HN (Lynds used the Grant HN only in the
    series of original paperback novels published by Belmont
    between 1963 and 1967.)

McCARTER, VER MILLE
  Jody McCarter: CPN

McCLARY, THOMAS CALVERT
  (See Nick Carter in Section IV.)
  Calvin Peregoy

McCOMAS, (Jesse) FRANCIS: b. 1910
  Webb Marlowe

McCULLEY, JOHNSTON: 1883-1958
  (See Nick Carter in Section IV.)
  Raley Brien
  George Drayne
  Frederick Phelps
  Rowena Raley
  Harrington Strong

McDANIEL, DAVID: 1939-1977
  Ted Johnstone

McDERMOTT, PAUL
  Dennis McDermott: CPN

McDONALD, EDWARD R.
  Raymond McDonald: CPN

MacDONALD, JOHN D(ann): b. 1916
  John Wade Farrell
  Robert Henry
  John Lane
  Scott O'Hara
  Peter Reed
  Henry Rieser

MacDONALD, PHILIP: b. 1899
  Oliver Fleming: CPN
  Martin Porlock

MacDONALD, RONALD
  Oliver Fleming: CPN

McFARLANE, LESLIE
  Franklin W. Dixon: SSN

McGAUGHY, DUDLEY (Dean)
  Dean Owen

McGIVERN, WILLIAM P(eter): b. 1924
  Alexander Blade: HN
  Bill Peters

MacGREGOR, JAMES M(urdock): b. 1925
  G.T. MacIntosh

McHARGUE, GEORGESS
  Alice Chase
  Margo Seesse Usher

MACHEN, ARTHUR: 1863-1947
  Gervase Perrot
  Leolinus Siluriensis

McHUGH, EDNA
  Kathleen Buddington Cox: CPN

McILWAIN, DAVID: b. 1921
  Charles Eric Maine
  Richard Rayner

MacINTOSH, ELIZABETH
  Gordon Daviot
  Josephine Tey

MacINTOSH, KENNETH
  Kent Casey

McINTOSH, KINN (Hamilton): b. 1930
  Catherine Aird

McKAY, MARY MINNIE: 1855-1924
  Marie Corelli

MacLEAN, ALISTAIR (Stuart)
  Ian Stuart

MacLEAN, KATHERINE: b. 1925
  Charles Dye (?) (Harold Sharp lists Dye as a PN; Donald
    Tuck lists Dye as a real person.)

McNEILE, H(erman) C(yril): 1888-1937
  Sapper (See also Gerard T. Farlie, Section I.)

MacNIE, JOHN: fl. c. 1883
  Ismar Thiusen

MAINWARING, DANIEL (Geoffrey Homes): 1902-1977
  Geoffrey Homes

MALZBURG, BARRY
  K.M. O'Donnell

MANN, GEORGE
  Arthur MacLean: HN (See Sexton Blake in Section IV.)

MANNING, ADELAIDE F.O.: 1891-1959
  Manning Coles: CPN
  Francis Gaite: CPN

MARSH, JOHN: b. 1907
  John Elton
  John Harley
  Harrington Hastings
  Grace Richmond
  Lillian Woodward

MARSHALL, EDISON (Tesla): 1894-1967
  Hall Hunter

MARTIN, F.H.
  Brian James Kelley: HN

MARTIN, R.A.
  E.C. Eliot

MARTIN, THOMAS H(ector): b. 1913
  Peter Saxon: HN
  Martin Thomas

MARTYN, EDWARD: fl. c. 1890
  Sirius

MASON, C.P.
  Epaminondas T. Snooks

MASON, DOUGLAS: b. 1918
  John Rankine

MASON, F(rancis) VAN WYCK: b. 1901
  Geoffrey Coffin
  Frank W. Mason
  Ward Weaver

MASON, PAMELA: b. 1915
  Pamela Kellino

MATHESON, RICHARD (Burton): b. 1926
  Logan Swanson

MATURIN, CHARLES (Robert): 1782-1824
  Jasper Dennis Murphy

MAXWELL, JOSLYN
  M.J. Ireland

MEEK, DORIS
  Gregory Mason: CPN

MEEK, CAPT. STERNER ST. PAUL: b. 1894
  Sterner St. Paul

MERCER, CECIL W.: fl. c. 1936
  Dornford Yates

MERRITT, A(braham): 1884-1943
  W. Fenimore

MERTZ, BARBARA: b. 1927
  Barbara Michaels

MERWIN, SAM, JR.: b. 1910
  Matt Lee
  Carter Sprague

METLOVA, MARIA: fl. c. 1940
  Louis Hathaway

MICHEL, JOHN: 1917-1969 ?
  Bowen Conway
  Arthur Cooke: CPN
  Hugh Raymond
  Lawrence Woods: CPN

MICHELS, NICHOLAS: fl. c. 1899
  Nikolai Mikalowitch

MILKOMANE, ALEXIS (Milkomanovich): b. 1903
  George Borodin
  George Sava

MILLAR, KENNETH: b. 1915
  John Macdonald
  John Ross Macdonald
  Ross Macdonald

MILLAR, ROBERT
  Whit Masterson: CPN
  Wade Miller: CPN

MILLER, P(eter) S(chuyler): 1912-1974
  Dennis McDermott: CPN
  Nihil

MONROE, DONALD
  Donald Keith: CPN

MONROE, KEITH
  Donald Keith: CPN

MONSELL, MRS. JOHN ROBERT
  Margaret Irwin

MONTAYNE, MONTE
  George Eaton: HN & CPN

MONTGOMERY, R(obert) B(ruce): 1921-1978
  Edmund Crispin

MOORCOCK, MICHAEL J(ohn): b. 1939
  Bill Barclay
  Edward P. Bradbury
  James Colvin
  Desmond Reid: HN (See Sexton Blake in Section IV.)

MOORE, C(atherine) L(ouise): b. 1911
  Keith Hammond: CPN
  Hudson Hastings: CPN
  C.H. Liddell: CPN
  Laurence O'Donnell: CPN
  Lewis Padgett: CPN

MORDAUNT, EVELYN M.: fl. c. 1930
  Elinor Mordaunt

MORRISON, PEGGY: d. 1973
  March Cost

MOSKOWITZ, SAM: b. 1920
  Robert Bahr
  Sam Martin
  Robert Sanders Shaw
  William M. Weiner
  Fred Wollonover

MOTT, J. MOLDON
  John Blackburn

MUDDOCK, JOYCE E.P.: 1843-1934
  Dick Donovan

MULLEN, STANLEY: 1911-1974
  Lee Beecher
  Stan Beecher
  John Peter Drummond: HN

MUNRO, H(ector) H(ugh): 1870-1916
  Saki

MURFREE, MARY (Noailles): fl. c. 1850
  Charles Egbert Craddock

MURRY, JOHN MIDDLETON: b. 1926
  Richard Cowper
  Colin Murry

MUSPRATT, ROSALIE: 1906-1976
  Jasper John

NEVILLE, KRIS: b. 1925
  Henderson Stark

NEWMAN, BERNARD: 1897-1968
  Don Betteridge

NEWMAN, JOHN
  Kenneth Johns: CPN

NICOLL, MAURICE: fl. c. 1918
  Martin Swayne

NISOT, MRS. MAVIS E.: fl. c. 1929
  William Penmare

NORRIS, EDWARD P.
  Zorro

NORTHRUP, EDWIN F.: fl. c. 1937
  Akkad Pseudoman

NORTON, ALICE MARY: b. 1912
  Andrew North
  Andre Norton
  Allen Weston

NORTON, ROGER HOWARD
  Robert C. Blackmon
  Robert Newman

NORWAY, NEVIL S(hute): 1899-1960
  Nevil Shute

NOWLAN, PHILIP F(rancis): 1881-1940
  Frank Phillips

NUETZEL, CHARLES A(lexander): b. 1934
  Charles English

NUTT, CHARLES: 1929-1967
  Charles Beaumont
  E.J. Beaumont
  Keith Grantland
  C.B. Lovehill
  Charles McNutt
  S.M. Tenneshaw: HN

NYE, NELSON CORAL: b. 1907
  Clem Colt
  Drake C. Denver
  Montague Rockingham

O'BRIEN, DAVID WRIGHT: d. 1944
  Alexander Blade: HN
  John York Cabot
  Bruce Dennis
  Duncan Farnesworth
  Clee Garson: HN
  Richard Vardon

ODELL, ERIC: 1862-1928
  Barry Pain

OFFUTT, ANDREW J.
  John Cleve

O'GRADY, STANDISH J.: fl. c. 1900
  Luke Netterfield
  Luke Netterville

OLDFIELD, CLAUDE (Houghton): fl. c. 1930
  Claude Houghton

OLSEN, ALFRED JOHN, JR.: 1884-1956
  Bob Olsen

OLSON, EUGENE E.: b. 1936
  Brad Steiger

O'MALLEY, MARY (Dolling): 1891-1974
  Ann Bridge

ONIONS, GEORGE OLIVER: 1874-1961
  (Although he legally changed his name to George Oliver, all
    of the writer's works appear under his original name of
    Oliver Onions.)

O NUALLAIN, BRIAN: 1911-1966
  Myles na Gopaleen
  Flann O'Brien
  Brian O Nolan

OPPENHEIM, E. PHILLIPS: 1866-1946
  Anthony Partridge

O'ROURKE, FRANK: b. 1916
  Frank O'Malley

OURSLER, CHARLES FULTON: 1893-1952
  Anthony Abbot

OVERHOLSER, WAYNE D.: b. 1906
  John S. Daniels
  Lee Leighton
  Wayne Roberts
  Dan J. Stevens
  Joseph Wayne

OWEN, HARRY C.: fl. c. 1924
  Hugh Addison

PAGE, NORVELL: 1904-1961
  Randolph Craig: HN
  Grant Stockbridge: HN

PAGET, VIOLET: 1856-1936
  Vernon Lee

PAINE, LAUREN: b. 1916
  Mark Carrell

PALMER, (Charles) STUART: 1905-1968
  Theodore Orchards
  Jay Stewart

PALMER, JOHN (Leslie)
  Francis Beeding: CPN

PALMER, RAYMOND A.: 1910-1977
  Henry Gade: HN
  G.H. Irwin: HN
  Frank Patton: HN
  Joe W(alter) Pelkie
  Wallace Quitman
  Alfred R. Steber: HN
  Morris J. Steele: HN
  Robert N. Webster
  Rae Winters

PALTOCK, ROBERT: 1697-1767
  R.S.

PANGBORN, EDGAR: 1909-1976
  Bruce Harrison

PARCELL, NORMAN H.: fl. c. 1948
  John Nicholson

PARGETER, EDITH: b. 1913
  Ellis Peters

PARTRIDGE, EDWARD (Bellamy): fl. c. 1935
  Thomas Bailey

PATTEN, LEWIS B(yford): b. 1915
  Lewis B. Ford

PATTEN, WILLIAM (Gilbert): 1866-1945
  Burt L. Standish: CPN

PAYES, RACHEL (Cosgrove): b. 1922
  E.L. Arch

PAYNE, DONALD GORDON: b. 1924
  Ian Cameron
  Donald Gordon
  James Vance Marshall

PEMBER-DEVEREUX, MARGARET R.: fl. c. 1938
  Roy Devereux

PENDLETON, DON
  Stephen Gregory

PENDRAY, EDWARD: b. 1901
  Gawain Edwards

PERKINS, VIOLET: fl. c. 1924
  William Leslie: CPN

PETAJA, EMIL: b. 1915
  Theodore Pine

PETERSILEA, CARLYLE: fl. c. 1893
  Ernst Von Himmel

PHELPS, GEORGE H.: fl. c. 1909
  Patrick Q. Tangent

PHILIPS, JUDSON (Pentecost): b. 1903
  Hugh Pentecost

PHILLIFENT, JOHN T.: 1916-1976
  John Rackham

PHILLIPS, DENNIS (John Andrew): b. 1924
  Peter Chambers
  Peter Chester

PHILLPOTS, EDEN: 1862-1960
  Herrington Hext

PHILPOT, JOSEPH (Henry): fl. c. 1900
  Philip LaFargue

PICTON, NINA: fl. c. 1893
  Laura Dearborn

PIERCE, JOHN: b. 1910
  J.J. Coupling

PIGGOTT, WILLIAM: fl. c. 1918
  Hubert Wales

PIM, HERBERT M.: fl. c. 1914
  A. Newman

PIRIE-GORDON, C.H.C.: b. 1912
  Prospero & Caliban: CPN

PITCAIRN, JOHN (James)
  Clifford Ashdown: CPN

PITTARD, HELENE: fl. c. 1926
  Noelle Roger

POHL, FREDERIK: b. 1919
  Elton V. Andrews
  Henry De Costa
  S.D. Gottesman: CPN
  Paul Dennis LaVond: CPN
  Edson McCann: CPN
  James MacCreigh
  Jordan Park: CPN
  Charles Satterfield: HN
  Alan Zweig

POLLOCK, JOHN: fl. c. 1918
  An Pilibin

PORTER, LINN B.: fl. c. 1890
  Albert Ross

POURNELLE, JERRY
  Wade Curtis

POWELL, TALMADGE: b. 1920
  Jack McCready

PRATT, FLETCHER: 1897-1956
  George U. Fletcher

PRATT, WILLIAM HENRY: 1887-1969
  Boris Karloff

PRICE, E(dgar) HOFFMAN: b. 1898
  Hamlin Daley

PRICHARD, HESKETH: 1876-1922
  E. & H. Heron: CPN

PRICHARD, KATE
  E. & H. Heron: CPN

PRITCHARD, JOHN
  Ian Wallace

PRITCHARD, WILLIAM (Thomas): b. 1909
  William Dexter

PRONZINI, WILLIAM
  Alex Saxon

QUILLER-COUCH, SIR ARTHUR: 1863-1944
  Q

RABE, ANN C.: fl. c. 1891
  Von Degen

RAMEY, BEN C.: d. 1977
  H.H. Hollis

RANDALL, GEORGIANA ANN: 1908-1957
  Michael Benning
  Craig Rice
  Daphne Sanders
  Michael Venning

RAPPOPORT, SOLOMON: fl. c. 1926
  S. Anskey

RATHBONE, ST. GEORGE
  See Section V

RAWSON, CLAYTON: 1906-1971
  Stewart Towne: HN

RAYMOND, RENE (Brabazon): b. 1906
  James Hadley Chase
  James Docherty
  Ambrose Grant
  Raymond Marshall

REED, ED
  Faith Lincoln: CPN

REEDS, F. ANTON
  Anthony Riker

REHM, WARREN S.: fl. c. 1898
  Omen Nemo

REICHNITZER, F.E.
  Lt. Scott Morgan: HN

RENTON, GERTRUDE: fl. c. 1926
  G. Colmore

REPP, ED EARL: b. 1901
  Bradner Buckner

RESSICH, JOHN: fl. c. 1928
  Gregory Baxter: CPN

REYNOLDS, DALLAS McCORD: b. 1917
  Mack Reynolds
  Maxine Reynolds
  Dallas Ross

REYNOLDS, WALTER D.: fl. c. 1898
  Lord Prime, Esq.

RICCI, LEWIS A.: fl. c. 1933
  Bartimeus

RICE, JANE
  Mary Austin (This is also the name of an author writing
    outside the science fiction-fantasy field.)

RICHARD, FRANÇOIS
  F. Richard-Bessiere: CPN

RICHARDSON, ROBERT S.: b. 1902
  Philip Latham

RICHTER, ERNST H.: 1901-1959
  William Brown
  Ernest Terridge

RIDING, LAURA
  Barbara Rich: CPN
  Madeleine Vara

RIDLEY, JAMES: fl. c. 1764
  Charles Morell

RIVETT, EDITH (Caroline)
  Carol Carnac
  E.C.R. Lorac

ROBERTS, KEITH: b. 1935
  John Kingston
  David Stringer

ROBERTSON, ALICE A.: fl. c. 1908
  Berthe St. Luz

ROBERTSON, FRANK (Chester): b. 1890
  Robert Crane
  Frank Chester Field
  King Hill

ROBINETT, STEPHEN
  Tak Hallus

ROCKLYNNE, ROSS: b. 1913
  H.F. Cente

RODDA, CHARLES: b. 1891
  Eliot Reed: CPN

ROE, IVAN: b. 1917
  Richard Savage

ROE, WILLIAM JAMES: fl. c. 1886
  Hudor Genone

ROGERS, WAYNE
  H.M. Appel
  Conrad Kimball

ROGOW, LEE
  Craig Ellis: HN

ROHR, WOLF (Detlef)
  Geff Caine
  Wayne Coover
  Alan Reed

ROLFE, FREDERICK WILLIAM: 1860-1913
  Baron Corvo
  Prospero & Caliban: CPN

ROLLINS, KATHLEEN
  Hal Debrett: CPN

ROLLINS, WILLIAM (Stacy Uran)
  O'Conner Stacy
  Urann Thayer

ROMANOFF, ALEXANDER (Nicholayevitch): 1881-1945
  Achmed Abdullah

ROSEWATER, FRANK: fl. c. 1920
  Marian & Franklin Mayon

ROSS, ALBERT: fl. c. 1932
  Frank Morison

ROSS, DAN
  Clarissa Ross
  Marilyn Ross

ROSSITER, JOHN: b. 1916
  Jonathan Ross

ROTH, HOLLY: 1916-1964
  K.G. Ballard
  P.J. Merrill

ROTHMAN, MILTON: b. 1919
  Lee Gregor

RUMBALL, CHARLES: fl. c. 1851
  Charles Delorme

RUSSELL, ERIC FRANK: b. 1905
  Webster Craig
  Morris J. Hugi (This was a real person. One story was
    accidentally credited to Russell under Hugi's name.)
  Duncan H. Munro

RUSSELL, GEORGE (William): 1867-1935
  AE

RYNAS, STEPHEN A.
  Stephen Arr

SABEN, GERTRUDE: fl. c. 1918
  Gregory Saben: CPN

ST. CLAIR, MARGARET: b. 1911
  William Hazel
  Idris Seabright

SAMACHSON, JOSEPH: b. 1906
  John Miller
  William Morrison
  Brett Sterling: HN

SAMPLINER, LOUIS H.
  Alexander Blade: HN

SANDERS, LEONARD M.: b. 1929
  Dan Thomas

SANDERSON, IVAN T.: 1911-1973
  Terence Roberts

SAUNDERS, HILARY (Aidan St. George)
  Francis Beeding: CPN

SAWYER, EUGENE T.: 1846-1924
  (See Nick Carter in Section IV.)

SAXON, RICHARD
  Henry Richards

SAYERS, DOROTHY L(eigh): 1893-1957
  Johanna Leigh

SCHACHNER, NATHEN
  Chan Corbett
  Walter Glamis

SCHEER, KARL (Herbert): b. 1928
  Alexai Turbojew

SCHER, MARIE: fl. c. 1915
  Marie Cher

SCHOEPFLIN, HARL (Vincent): 1893-1968
  Harl Vincent

SCHOPFER, JEAN: fl. c. 1927
  Claude Anet

SCORTIA, THOMAS N(icholas): b. 1926
  Arthur R. Kurz
  Gerald McDow
  Scott Nichols

SCOTT, PEGGY O.
  Barton Werper: CPN

SCOTT, PETER T.
  Barton Werper: CPN

SCOTT, R(eginald) T. M(aitland)
  Brant House: HN

SCOTT, ROBERT: fl. c. 1921
  Blue Wolf

SCOTT, SIR WALTER: 1771-1832
  Jedediah Cleishbotham

SENARENS, LUIS (Philip): 1863-1939
  Kit Clyde
  W.J. Earle
  Police Captain Howard
  Noname
  Ned Sparling

SERNER, MARTIN G.: fl. c. 1925
  Frank Heller

SEYMOUR, FREDERICK H.: fl. c. 1898
  Lord Gilhooley

SHARP, WILLIAM: 1856(?)-1905
  Fiona MacLeod
  H.P. Siwaarmill

SHAVER, RICHARD S.: 1907-1975
  Wes Amhurst
  Edwin Benson (This was the name of a real person. The name
    was used once as a PN by mistake.)
  Alexander Blade: HN
  Peter Dexter
  G.H. Irwin: HN
  Paul Lohman: HN
  Frank Patton: HN
  Stan Raycraft
  D. Richard Sharpe

SHECKLEY, ROBERT E.: b. 1928
  Phillips Barbee
  Finn O'Donnevan

SHELDON, ALICE
  Racoona Sheldon
  James Tiptree, Jr.

SHELDON, WALTER J.: b. 1917
  Seldon Walters

SHELLABARGER, SAMUEL: fl. c. 1930
  John Estevan

SHEPARD, WILSON
  Willis W. Woe

SHERMAN, FRANK (Dempster): 1860-1916
  Two Wags: CPN

SHIEL, M.P.: 1865-1947
  Carton Arliss
  Charles Arliss
  Stephanie Belamy
  Gordon Holmes: CPN
  N.R. Shean
  Louis Tracy (Shiel wrote Chapters XXIX-XXXIX in Tracy's *An
    American Emperor*, published in 1897, but received no
    credit for them.)
  (The names Belamy, Shean and Carton and Charles Arliss exist
    in manuscripts, but may not have appeared in published
    sources as of this writing. Verifications for these are
    in A. Reynolds Morse, *M.P. Shiel, the Man & His Works*;
    see SOURCES.)

SHIRAS, WILMAR H.: b. 1908
  Jane Howes

SHROYER, FREDERICK
  Erick Freyer

SIEGEL, JEROME: b. 1914
  Bernard J. Kenton

SILBERBERG, MRS. WILLIAM
  Lesley F. Stone

SILVERBERG, ROBERT: b. 1936
  Gordon Aghill: HN
  Robert Arnett: HN
  T.D. Bethlen
  Alexander Blade: HN
  Ralph Burke: HN
  Walker Chapman
  Dirk Clinton
  Randall Garett
  Richard Greer: HN
  E.K. Jarvis: HN
  Ivar Jorgensen: HN
  Waren Kastel: HN
  Calvin M. Knox
  Ray McKenzie
  Dan Malcolm
  Webber Martin
  Alex Merriman
  Clyde Mitchell: HN

SILVERBERG, ROBERT (cont'd)
  David Osborne
  George Osborne
  Robert Randall: CPN
  Eric Rodman
  Lee Sebastian
  Leonard G. Spencer: HN
  S.M. Tenneshaw: HN
  Hall Thornton
  Gerold Vance: HN
  Richard F. Watson

SILVETTE, HENRY: b. 1907
  Barnaby Dogbolt

SIMENON, GEORGES (-Joseph-Christian): b. 1903
  Christian Brulls
  Georges Caraman
  Germain D'Antibes
  Jacques Dersonne
  Georges D'Isly
  Jean Dorsage
  Luc Dorsan
  Jean Dossage
  Jean DuPerry
  Georges Martin Georges
  Monsieur LeCoq

SIMPSON, WILLIAM: fl. c. 1891
  Thomas Blot

SIMSON, ERIC (Andrew)
  Laurence Kirk

SINIHSVSKII, ANDREI (Donatevich): b. 1925
  Abram Tertz

SKINNER, CONRAD A.: fl. c. 1923
  Michael Maurice

SKINNER, JUNE (O'Grady): b. 1922
  Rohan O'Grady

SLADEK, JOHN T.: b. 1937
  Thom Demijohn: CPN

SLATER, ERNEST: fl. c. 1910
  Paul Gwynne

SLESAR, HENRY: b. 1927
  O.H. Leslie

SLOTKIN, JOSEPH
  Oliver Spie
  Nick Tolz

SMALL, AUSTIN: d. 1929
  Seamark

SMITH, CLARK ASHTON: 1893-1961
  Timeus Gaylord

SMITH, DODIE
  C.L. Anthony

SMITH, ELIZABETH (Thomasina Meade): fl. c. 1903
  L.T. Meade

SMITH, ERNEST (Bramah): 1869-1942
  Ernest Bramah

SMITH, GEORGE H.
  M.J. Deer: CPN

SMITH, GEORGE O.: b. 1911
  Wesley Long

SMITH, L.H.: b. 1916
  Speedy Williams

SMITH, RON(ald Loran): b. 1936
  Martin Loran: CPN

SMOLARSKI, MR. & MRS.
  Henry Damonti: CPN

SNEDDON, ROBERT W.: 1880-1944
  Robert Guillaume
  Mark Shadow

SOUTHWOLD, STEPHEN: 1887-1964
  Neil Bell
  S.H. Lambert
  Paul Martens
  Miles

SPICER, BART: b. 1918
  Jay Barbette: CPN

SPICER, BETTY
  Jay Barbette: CPN

SPOTSWOOD, DILLON (Jordan): fl. c. 1901
  Nuverbis

SQUIRE, SIR JOHN COLLINGS: 1882-1958
  Solomon Eagle

STANDISH, ROBERT
  Digby George Gerahty

STEARNS, ALBERT: fl. c. 1904
  Edgar Franklin

STEELE, MARY QUINTARD: b. 1922
  Wilson Gage

STERLING, STEWART
  G. Wayman Jones: HN

STEVENS, LAWRENCE (Sterne)
  Lawrence

STEVENSON, JOHN: fl. c. 1903
  Stephen Jackson

STEWART, ALFRED (Walter): 1880-1947
  J.J. Connington
  John Jervis Connington

STEWART, JOHN (Innes Mackintosh): b. 1906
  Michael Innes

STICKLER, CHARLES A.: fl. c. 1933
  Brogan the Scribe

STICKNEY, CORWIN
  Philip Sutter

STINE, G. HARRY: b. 1928
  Lee Correy

STORY, A.M. SOMMERVILLE: fl. c. 1907
  Frankfort Sommerville

STOWE, MRS. H.M.: fl. c. 1890
  Eleve

STRATEMEYER, EDWARD L.: 1862-1930
  (See Section V, Stratemeyer Syndicate Names.)

STREET, CECIL (John Charles): b. 1884
  Miles Burton
  F.O.O.
  John Rhode
  X.X.

STUBBS, HARRY C(lement): b. 1922
  Hal Clement

STURGEON, THEODORE (Hamilton): b. 1918
  (Born Edward Hamilton Waldo, he legally changed his name
    to Theodore Hamilton Sturgeon.)
  Frederick R. Ewing
  E. Waldo Hunter
  E. Hunter Waldo

SUDDABY, WILLIAM (Donald): b. 1900
  Alan Griff

SUTTON, GRAHAM: fl. c. 1930
  Anthony Marsden

SWAIN, DWIGHT V(reeland): b. 1915
  Clark South

SWIFT, JONATHAN: 1667-1745
  Isaac Bickerstaff
  Lemuel Gulliver

SWINTON, SIR ERNEST DUNLOP: 1868-1951
  Ole Luk-Oie

SYMMES, JOHN CLEAVES: 1780-1829
  Capt. Adam Seaborn

TAIT, GEORGE B.
  Alan Barclay

TAYLOR, PHOEBE ATWOOD: 1909-1976
  Alice Tilton

TEED, C(yrus) R(eed): fl. c. 1909
  Lord Chester

TEPPERMAN, EMIL
  Kenneth Robeson: HN
  Curtis Steele: HN

THAYER, TIFFANY (Ellsworth): b. 1902
  John Doe
  Elmer Ellsworth, Jr.
  Tiffany Thayer

THIBEAULT, JACQUES-ANATOLE (François): 1844-1924
  Anatole France

THOMAS, ELIZABETH: fl. c. 1812
  Bridget Bluemantle

THOMAS, THEODORE L.: b. 1920
  Leonard Lockhard

THOMPSON, ANTHONY A.
  Antony Alban

THOMSON, C(hristine) C(ampbell): b. 1897 ?
  Christine Hartley
  Flavia Richardson

THOMSON, W.: fl. c. 1783
  A Man of the People

TILLOTSON, JOE W.
  Robert Fuqua

TINSLEY, THEODORE
  Maxwell Grant: HN

TODD, RUTHVEN: b. 1914
  R.T. Campbell

TOOKER, RICHARD
  Henry E. Lemke

TORSVAN, TRAVEN: 1890-1969
  B. Traven

TOURGEE, ALBION WINEGAR: 1838-1905
  Edgar Henry

TOWLE, MRS. A.E.
  Margery Lawrence

TRACY, LOUIS: 1863-1928
  Gordon Holmes: CPN
  (See also M.P. Shiel in Section I.)

TRACY, ROGER S.
  Shirby T. Hodge

TREMAINE, F. ORLIN: 1899-1956
  Anne Beale
  Arthur Lane
  Guthrie Payne
  Warren B. Sand
  Alfred Santos
  Warner Van Lorne

TRENERY, GLADYS (Gordon): 1885?-1938
  G.G. Pendarves

TREVOR, ELLESTON: b. 1920
  Adam Hall

TUBB, E(dwin) C(harles): b. 1919
  Ted Bain
  Charles Gray
  Volstead Gridban
  Alan Guthrie
  Gill Hunt
  Gregory Kern
  Duncan Lamont
  King Lang (This PN was also used independently by John
    Russell Fearn.)
  Arthur MacLean: HN (See Sexton Blake in Section IV.)
  Carl Maddox
  Philip Martyn
  Gavin Neal
  Brian Shaw
  Roy Sheldon

88

TUCKER, CHARLOTTE: 1821-1893
  A.L.O.E.

TUCKER, GEORGE: 1775-1861
  Joseph Atterley

TUCKER, NATHANIEL (Beverley): 1784-1851
  Edward William Sidney

UNWIN, DAVID STORR: b. 1918
  David Severn

UPCHURCH, BOYD: b. 1919
  John Boyd

VAIRASSE, DENIS: fl. c. 1674
  Captain Siden

VANCE, JOHN (Holbrook): b. 1916
  Jack Vance

VANCEL, DORIS
  Doris Thomas

VAUGHAN, AURIEL R.: fl. c. 1946
  Oriel Malet

VAUX, PATRICK: fl. c. 1907
  Navarchus: CPN

VENABLE, CLARK: fl. c. 1932
  Covington Clarke

VERN, DAVID: b. 1924
  Alexander Blade (This was originally a personal PN of
    Vern's; later it became a HN.)
  Craig Ellis: HN
  Peter Horn: HN
  David V. Reed
  Clyde Woodruff

VERNON, GEORGE S.G.: fl. c. 1939
  Vernon George

VERRAL, CHUCK
  George Eaton: HN & CPN

VERRIL, A(lpheus) HYATT: 1871-1954
  Ray Ainsbury

VERSACK, MARIA (Theresa Rios): b. 1917
  Tere Rios

VIARD, HENRI
  Henry Ward

VICKERS, ROY: 1899-1965
  David Durham
  Sefton Kyle
  John Spencer

VIDAL, GORE: b. 1925
  Edgar Box

VIVIAN, E. CHARLES: 1882-1947
  Jack Mann

VLASTO, J.A.
  John Remenham

VOELKE, JOHN (Donaldson)
  Robert Traver

WADE, ROBERT
  Whit Masterson: CPN
  Wade Miller: CPN

WALL, JOHN W.
  Sarban

WALLER, LESLIE: b. 1923
  C.S. Cody

WALLIS, G. McDONALD
  Hope Campbell

WALLIS, GEORGE C.
  John Stanton

WALSH, JAMES MORGEN: 1897-1952
  H. Haverstock Hill
  Stephen Maddock

WALTON, BRYCE: b. 1918
  Paul Franklin
  Kenneth O'Hara
  Dave Sands: HN

WALTON, HARRY
  Harry Collier

WANDREI, HOWARD E(lmer): 1909-1956
  Robert Coley
  Robert A. Garron
  Howard Grahame
  H.W. Guernsey
  Howard VonDrey

WARD, ARTHUR (Salsfield): 1883-1959
  Michael Furey
  Sax Rohmer

WARD, HAROLD
  Zorro: HN

WARD, ROSE (Elizabeth Knox): b. 1886
  Lisbeth Knox
  Elizabeth Sax Rohmer

WARDE, BEATRICE (Lamberton): fl. c. 1937
  Paul Beaujon

WARNER, K(enneth) L(ewis): b. 1918
  Dighton Morel

WAYNE, CHARLES (Stokes): b. 1858
  Horace Hazeltine

WEAVER, GERTRUDE: fl. c. 1926
  Gertrude C. Dunn

WEBB, RICHARD
  Q. Patrick: CPN
  Patrick Quentin: CPN
  Jonathan Stagg: CPN

WEINBAUM, STANLEY G(rauman): 1912-1935
  John Jessel
  Marge Stanley

WEISINGER, MORT: b. 1915
  Will Garth: HN
  Tom Irwin Geris

WEISS, GEORGE HENRY: 1898-1946
  Francis Flagg

WELCH, EDGAR L.: fl. c. 1882
  Grip

WELLMAN, BERT J.: fl. c. 1898
  A Law-Abiding Revolutionist

WELLMAN, MANLY WADE: b. 1903
  Gabriel Barclay
  Levi Crow
  Gans T. Field

WELLMAN, MRS. MANLY WADE
  Frances Garfield

WELLS, ANGUS
  J.B. Dancer: HN
  Ian Evans
  Charles C. Garrett: HN
  Richard Kirk: HN
  James A. Muir
  Charles R. Pike: HN

WELLS, BASIL: b. 1912
  Gene Ellerman

WERTENBAKER, G. PAYTON: b. 1907
  Green Payton

WESTLAKE, DONALD E(dwin): b. 1933
  Curt Clark
  Tucker Coe
  Timothy J. Culver
  J. Morgan Cunningham
  Richard Stark

WHEELER, HUGH C.
  Q. Patrick: CPN
  Patrick Quentin: CPN
  Jonathan Stagg: CPN

WHITE, TED: b. 1938
  Norman Edwards: CPN

WHITE, T(erence) H(anbury): 1906-1964
  James Aston

WHITE, WILLIAM (Anthony Parker): 1911-1968
  Anthony Boucher
  H.H. Holmes
  Herman W. Mudgett
  Parker White

WHITSON, JOHN HARVEY: 1854-1936
  Luke Garland
  Capt./Col. Hazelton
  Frank Merriwell
  Arthur Sewell
  Lt. A.K. Sims
  Burt Standish: CPN
  Addison Steele
  Robert Steele
  Maurice Stevens
  Russell Williams
  (See also Nick Carter in Section IV.)

WHITTINGTON, HARRY: b. 1915
  Whit Harrison
  Kel Holland
  Harriet Kathryn Myers
  Steve Phillips
  Clay Stuart
  Hondo Wells
  Harry White
  Hallam Whitney

WIBBERLEY, LEONARD (Patrick O'Connor): b. 1915
  Leonard Holton
  Patrick O'Connor

WICKER, THOMAS: b. 1926
  Paul Connolly

WIENER, NORBERT: 1894-1964
  W. Norbert

WILCOX, DON: b. 1908
  Buzz-Bolt Atomcracker
  Alexander Blade: HN
  Cleo Eldon
  Max Overton
  Miles Shelton

WILDING, PHILIP
  John Robert Haynes

WILKINSON, LOUIS W.: fl. c. 1944
  Louis Marlowe

WILLIAMS, ROBERT MOORE: b. 1907
  John S. Browning
  H.H. Harmon
  E.K. Jarvis: HN
  Robert Moore
  Russell Storm

WILLIAMS, ROSWELL: 1893-1968
  Frank Owen
  Hung Long Tom

WILLIAMS, THOMAS (Lanier): b. 1914
  Tennessee Williams

WILLIAMSON, ETHEL: fl. c. 1932
  Jane Cardinal

WILLIAMSON, JACK: b. 1908
  Will Stewart

WILLIS, A(nthony) A(rmstrong): b. 1897
  Anthony Armstrong

WILLIS, WALTER
  Walter Ryan

WILSON, JOHN (Anthony Burgess): b. 1917
  Anthony Burgess
  Joseph Kell
  John Burgess Wilson

WILSON, RICHARD: b. 1920
  Ivor Towers: HN

WINTERBOTHAM, RUSS: 1904-1971
  Ted Addy
  J. Harvey Bond
  Franklin Hadley
  R.R. Winter

WOLLHEIM, DON: b. 1914
  Arthur Cooke: CPN
  Millard Verne Gordon
  David Grinnell
  Martin Pearson
  Allen Warland
  Braxton Welles
  Willy the Wisp
  Lawrence Woods: CPN & PN
  "X"

WOODARD, WAYNE: 1914-1964
  Hannes Bok
  Dolbokov: CPN

WOODFORD, JACK: 1894-1971
  Josiah Pitts Woolfolk

WOOLRICH, CORNELL: 1903(?)-1968
  George Hopley
  William Irish

WORMSER, RICHARD (Edward): 1908-1977
  (See Nick Carter in Section IV.)

WORRELL, EVERIL: 1893-1969
  Lireve Monett

WORTS, GEORGE FRANK: b. 1892
  Loring Brent

WRIGHT, FARNSWORTH: 1888-1940
  Francis Hard

WRIGHT, MABEL OSGOOD: fl. c. 1859
  Barbara

WRIGHT, NOEL: fl. c. 1924
  Nigel Worth

WRIGHT, SEWELL PEASELEY: 1897-1970
  Thomas Andrews
  Leigh Cameron
  Parke Spencer

WRIGHT, SYDNEY FOWLER: 1874-1965
  Sydney Fowler
  Allen Seymour

WRIGHT, WILLARD (Huntington): 1888-1965
  S.S. Van Dine

WROSZ, JOSEPH
  Joseph Ross

WYBRANIEC, PETER F.: fl. c. 1935
  Raphael W. Leonhart

YERXA, LEROY: 1915-1946
  Alexander Blade: HN
  Richard Casey

YEXLEY, LIONEL
  Navarchus: CPN

YOUD, CHRISTOPHER: b. 1922
  John Christopher

ZACHERLE, JOHN: b. 1919
  Zackerley

ZAGAT, ARTHUR LEO: 1895-1948
  Brant House: HN

ZIEGLER, EDWARD W.: b. 1932
  Theodore Tyler

SECTION II

PEN NAMES OR PSEUDONYMS (PN)

These are defined as the private writing names of
the individual writers. This section lists each
PN alphabetically, followed by the real name (RN)
of the writer.

A, DR.
  RN: Isaac Asimov

A.L.O.E.
  RN: Charlotte Tucker

ABBOTT, ANTHONY
  RN: Charles Fulton Oursler

ABDULLAH, ACHMED
  RN: Alexander Nicholayevitch Romanoff

ACRE, STEPHEN
  RN: Frank Gruber

ACULA, DR.
  RN: Forrest J. Ackerman

ADAIR, DENNIS
  RN: Bernard Cronin

ADAMS, JACK
  RN: Alcanoan O. Grigsby

ADDISON, HUGH
  RN: Harry C. Owen

ADDY, TED
  RN: Russ Winterbotham

ADELER, MAX
  RN: Charles H. Clark

ADEPT, AN
  RN: Charles Johnstone

AE
  RN: George William Russell

AGAR, BRIAN
  RN: Willis Todhunter Ballard

AGRICOLA, SYLVIUS
  RN: Forrest J. Ackerman

AGUECHEEK
  RN: Charles Bullard Fairbanks

AHEARNE, BURT
  RN: Albert Hernhuter

AINSBURY, RAY
  RN: A. Hyatt Verral

AIRD, CATHERINE
  RN: Kinn Hamilton McIntosh

AKERS, FLOYD
  RN: L. Frank Baum

ALAN, A.J.
  RN: Leslie H. Lambert

Al ARAWIYAH
  RN: H.N. Crellin

ALBAN, ANTONY
  RN: Anthony A. Thompson

ALBRAND, MARTHA
  RN: Heidi Huberta Freybe

ALLEN, F.M.
  RN: Edmund Downey

ALLISON, SAM
  RN: Noel Loomis

ALLPORT, ARTHUR
  RN: Raymond Z. Gallun

ALVAREZ, JOHN
  RN: Lester del Rey

AMES, CLINTON
  RN: Roger P. Graham

AMHURST, WES
  RN: Richard S. Shaver

AMOS, ALAN
  RN: K.N. Knight

ANDERSON, DAVID
  RN: Raymond F. Jones

ANDERSON, KAREN
  RN: June Millichamp Kruse

ANDOM, R.
  RN: Alfred W. Barrett

ANDREW, STEPHEN
  RN: Frank George Layton

ANDREWS, ELTON V.
  RN: Frederik Pohl

ANDREWS, THOMAS
  RN: Sewell Peaseley Wright

ANDREZEL, PIERRE
  RN: Baroness Karen Blixen

ANET, CLAUDE
  RN: Jean Schopfer

ANSKEY, S.
  RN: Solomon Rappoport

ANSTEY, F.
  RN: Thomas A. Guthrie

ANTHONY, C.L.
  RN: Dodie Smith

ANVIL, CHRISTOPHER
  RN: Harry C. Crosby

APPEL, H.M.
  RN: Wayne Rogers

APPLETON, LAWRENCE
  RN: H.P. Lovecraft

ARCH, E.L.
  RN: Rachel Cosgrove Payes

ARCHER, A.A.
  RN: Archie L. Joscelyn

ARCHETT, GUY
  RN: Chester S. Geier

ARCOT, ROGER
  RN: Robert Donald Locke

ARDEN, WILLIAM
  RN: Dennis Lynds

ARLEN, MICHAEL
  RN: Dikran Kouyoumdjian

ARLISS, CARTON
  RN: M.P. Shiel

ARLISS, CHARLES
  RN: M.P. Shiel

ARMSTRONG, ANTHONY
  RN: Anthony Armstrong Willis

ARMSTRONG, GEOFFREY
  RN: John Russell Fearn

ARNOLD, JOHN
  RN: Frederick Arnold Kummer

ARR, STEPHEN
  RN: Stephen A. Rynas

ASH, FENTON
  RN: Frank Aubray

ASHE, GORDON
  RN: John Creasey

ASHTON, WARREN T.
  RN: William T. Adams

ASKHAM, FRANCIS
  RN: Julia Greenwood

ASQUITH, LADY CYNTHIA
  RN: Mary Evelyn Charteris

ASTON, JAMES
  RN: T.H. White

ATHELING, WILLIAM, JR.
  RN: James Blish

ATKINS, FRANK
  RN: Frank Aubray

ATTERLEY, JOSEPH
  RN: George Tucker

AUNT NAOMI
  RN: Gertrude Landa

AUSTIN, FRANK
  RN: Frederick Faust

AUSTIN, MARY
  RN: Jane Rice (See Jane Rice in Section I.)

AVERY, RICHARD
  RN: Edmund Cooper

AYERS, PAUL
  RN: Edward S. Aarons

AYRE, THORNTON
  RN: John Russell Fearn

AYSCOUGH, JOHN
  RN: Francis B. Bickerstaffe-Drew

BADGER, RICHARD C.
  RN: Eric Temple Bell

BAHR, ROBERT
  RN: Sam Moskowitz

BAILEY, THOMAS
  RN: Edward Bellamy Partridge

BAIN, TED
  RN: E.C. Tubb

BAKER, ASA
  RN: Davis Dresser

BALBOA, S.F.
  RN: Forrest J. Ackerman

BALLARD, K.G.
  RN: Holly Roth

BALLARD, P.D.
  RN: Willis Todhunter Ballard

BALLARD, W.T.
  RN: Willis Todhunter Ballard

BALLARD, WILLIS T.
  RN: Willis Todhunter Ballard

BALLINGER, BILL S.
  RN: William S. Ballinger

BANAT, D.R.
  RN: Ray Bradbury

BANCROFT, LAURA
  RN: L. Frank Baum

BARBARA
  RN: Mabel O. Wright

BARBEE, PHILLIPS
  RN: Robert Sheckley

BARCLAY, ALAN
  RN: George B. Tait

BARCLAY, BENNETT
  RN: Kendall Foster Crossen

BARCLAY, BILL
  RN: Michael J. Moorcock

BARCLAY, GABRIEL
  RN: Manly Wade Wellman

BARCZYNKA, HELENE
  RN: Marguerite F. Barclay

BARNABY, HUGO
  RN: Ernest H. Fitzpatrick

BARNES, DAVE
  RN: Arthur K. Barnes

BARONTE, GERVE
  RN: Baronte Gervee

BARRETON, GRANDALL
  RN: Randall Garrett

BARRINGTON, E.
  RN: Lily Adams Beck

BARSHOFSKY, PHILIP
  RN: Philip J. Bartel

BARTIMEUS
  RN: Lewis A. Ricci

BARTON, ERLE
  RN: R.L. Fanthorpe

BAXTER, GEORGE OWEN
  RN: Frederick Faust

BEAL, NICK
  RN: Forrest J. Ackerman

BEALE, ANNE
  RN: F. Orlin Tremaine

BEAN, NORMAN
  RN: Edgar Rice Burroughs

BEARDON, ANTHONY
  RN: Paul Linebarger

BEAUJON, PAUL
  RN: Beatrice Lamberton Warde

BEAUMONT, CHARLES
  RN: Charles Nutt

BEAUMONT, E.J.
  RN: Charles Nutt

BECHDOLT, JACK
  RN: John Ernest Bechdolt

BECK, ALLEN
  RN: Hugh B. Cave

BECK, CHRISTOPHER
  RN: Thomas C. Bridges

BEDFORD-JONES, H.
  RN: Henry James O'Brien Bedford-Jones

BEECHER, LEE
  RN: Stanley Mullen

BEECHER, STAN
  RN: Stanley Mullen

BEHAN, LESLIE
  RN: Theodore Mark Gottfried

BELAMY, STEPHANIE
  RN: M.P. Shiel

BELL, NEIL
  RN: Stephen Southwold

BENNING, MICHAEL
  RN: Georgiana Ann Randall

BERKELEY, ANTHONY
  RN: Anthony Berkeley Cox

BETHLEN, T.D.
  RN: Robert Silverberg

BETTERIDGE, DON
  RN: Bernard Newman

BEYNON, JOHN
  RN: John Beynon Harris

BICKERSTAFF, ISAAC
  RN: Jonathan Swift

BICKERSTAFF, ISAAC, JR.
  RN: H.P. Lovecraft

BINGHAM, CARSON
  RN: Bruce Cassiday

BIRD, CORTWAINER
  RN: Harlan Ellison

BLACKBURN, JOHN
  RN: J. Molden Mott

BLACKMON, ROBERT C.
  RN: Roger Howard Norton

BLAINE, JAMES
  RN: Michael Avallone

BLAIR, HAMISH
  RN: Andrew J. Blair

BLAKE, NICHOLAS
  RN: Cecil Day-Lewis

BLAYN, HUGO
  RN: John Russell Fearn

BLAYRE, CHRISTOPHER
  RN: Edward Heron-Allen

BLOOD, MATTHEW
  RN: Davis Dresser

BLOODSTONE, JOHN
  RN: Stuart James Byrne

BLOT, THOMAS
  RN: William Simpson

BLUEMANTEL, BRIDGET
  RN: Elizabeth Thomas

BLUE WOLF
  RN: Robert Scott

BOISGILBERT, EDMUND
  RN: Ignatius Donnelly

BOK, HANNES
  RN: Wayne Woodard

BOLT, LEE
  RN: Frederick Faust

BOND, J. HARVEY
  RN: Russ Winterbotham

BONNER, PARKER
  RN: Willis Todhunter Ballard

BOOK, PENDLETON
  RN: Poul Anderson

BOOTH, IRWIN
  RN: Edward D. Hoch

BORODIN, GEORGE
  RN: Alexis Milkomanovich Milkomane

BOSTON, CHARLES K.
  RN: Frank Gruber

BOTTSFORD, LORD
  RN: James Dennis Hird

BOUCHER, ANTHONY
  RN: William Anthony Parker White

BOWEN, MARJORIE
  RN: Gabrielle Campbell

BOWIE, SAM
  RN: Willis Todhunter Ballard

BOX, EDGAR
  RN: Gore Vidal

BOYCE, MORTON
  RN: John Russell Fearn

BOYD, JOHN
  RN: Boyd Upchurch

BRADBURY, EDWARD P.
  RN: Michael J. Moorcock

BRAMAH, ERNEST
  RN: Ernest Bramah Smith

BRAND, CHRISTINA
  RN: Mary Christina Lewis

BRAND, MAX
  RN: Frederick Faust

BREHAT, ALFRED
  RN: Alfred Guezenec

BRENT, LORING
  RN: George Frank Worts

BRETT, LEO
  RN: Robert Lionel Fanthorpe

BRIARTON, GRENDEL
  RN: Reginald Bretnor

BRIDGE, ANN
  RN: Mary Dolling O'Malley

BRIDGE, FRANK J.
  RN: Francis J. Brueckel

BRIDGER, JOHN
  RN: Joe Gibson

BRIEN, RALEY
  RN: Johnstone McCulley

BROGAN, JAMES
  RN: Christopher Hodder-Williams

BROGAN THE SCRIBE
  RN: Charles A. Stickler

BROOKER, CLARK
  RN: Kenneth Fowler

BROUGHTON, PHILIP
  RN: Aubrey Beardsley

BROWN, IRVING
  RN: William T. Adams

BROWN, JOHN
  RN: Willy Ley

BROWN, WILLIAM
  RN: Ernst H. Richter

BROWNING, CRAIG
  RN: Roger P. Graham

BROWNING, JOHN S.
  RN: Robert Moore Williams

BRUCE, LEO
  RN: Rupert Croft-Cooke

BRULLS, CHRISTIAN
  RN: Georges Simenon

BRUNNER, K. HOUSTON
  RN: John K.H. Brunner

BRYANT, PETER
  RN: Peter George

BUCKNER, BRADNER
  RN: Ed Earl Repp

BUCKROSE, J.E.
  RN: Annie E. Jameson

BUDRYS, ALGIS
  RN: Algirdas Jonas Budrys

BUNTLINE, NED
  RN: E.Z.C. Judson

BURFORD, ELEANOR
  RN: Eleanor Burford Hibbert

BURGESS, ANTHONY
  RN: John Anthony Burgess Wilson

BURTON, MILES
  RN: Cecil John Charles Street

BUTLER, WALTER G.
  RN: Frederick Faust

BUXTON, CARL
  RN: Harold Hersey

BUZZ-BOLT ATOMCRACKER
  RN: Don Wilcox

CABELL, BRANCH
  RN: James Branch Cabell

CABOT, JOHN YORK
  RN: David Wright O'Brien

CAINE, GEFF
  RN: Wolf Detlef Rohr

CAIRNES, MAUD
  RN: Kathleen H. Curzon-Herrick

CALLAHAN, WILLIAM
  RN: Raymond Z. Gallun

CAMERON, IAN
  RN: Donald Gordon Payne

CAMPBELL, CLYDE CRAIN
  RN: H.L. Gold

CAMPBELL, HOPE
  RN: G. McDonald Wallis

CAMPBELL, R.T.
  RN: Ruthven Todd

CAMPEN, KARL van
  RN: John W. Campbell, Jr.

CANNON, CURT
  RN: S.A. Lombino

CARAMAN, GEORGES
  RN: Georges Simenon

CARDINAL, JANE
  RN: Ethel Williamson

CARGHILL, RALPH
  RN: Arthur Jean Cox

CARLISLE, CLARK
  RN: James Clark Carlisle Holding, Jr.

CARNAC, CAROL
  RN: Edith Caroline Rivett

CARR, PHILIPPA
  RN: Eleanor Burford Hibbert

CARRELL, MARK
  RN: Lauren Paine

CARROLL, LEWIS
  RN: Charles Lutwig Dodgson

CARSAC, FRANCIS
  RN: François Bordes

CASEY, KENT
  RN: Kent MacIntosh

CASEY, RICHARD
  RN: Leroy Yerxa

CASH, HARMON
  RN: Lester Dent

CASSIUS
  RN: Michael Foot

CASTLE, ROBERT
  RN: Edmund Hamilton

CAVENDISH, PETER
  RN: Sydney Horler

CECIL, HENRY
  RN: David H. Keller

CENTE, H.F.
  RN: Ross Rocklynne

CHABER, M.E.
  RN: Kendall Foster Crossen

CHAIN, JULAIN
  RN: May Dikty

CHALLIS, GEORGE
  RN: Frederick Faust

CHAMBERLAIN, WILLIAM
  RN: Dale C. Donaldson

CHAMBERS, DANA
  RN: Albert Leffingwell

CHAMBERS, PETER
  RN: Dennis J.A. Phillips

CHAPMAN, WALKER
  RN: Robert Silverberg

CHARLES, FRANKLIN
  RN: Cleve Franklin Adams

CHARLOT, HENRY
  RN: Walter D. Gibson

CHARTERIS, LESLIE
  RN: Leslie C.B. Lin

CHASE, ALICE
  RN: Georgess McHargue

CHASE, BORDEN
  RN: Frank Fowler

CHASE, JAMES HADLEY
  RN: Rene Raymond

CHEIRO
  RN: Louis Hamon

CHER, MARIE
  RN: Marie Scher

CHESTER, LORD
  RN: C(yrus) R(eed) Teed

CHESTER, PETER
  RN: Dennis J.A. Phillips

CHRISTOPHER, JOHN
  RN: Christopher Youd

CLARK, BADGER
  RN: Charles Badger Clark

CLARK, CURT
  RN: Donald E. Westlake

CLARK, DALE
  RN: Ronal Kayser

CLARK, GEORGE E.
  RN: Ronal Kayser

CLARKE, COVINGTON
  RN: Clark Venable

CLAY, CHARLES M.
  RN: Charlotte M. Clark

CLEISHBOTHAM, JEDEDIAH
  RN: Sir Walter Scott

CLEMENT, HAL
  RN: Harry Clement Stubbs

CLEVE, JOHN
  RN: Andrew J. Offutt

CLINTON, DIRK
  RN: Robert Silverberg

CLIVE, DENNIS
  RN: John Russell Fearn

CLYDE, KIT
  RN: Luis Philip Senarens

CODY, AL
  RN: Archie L. Joscelyn

CODY, C.S.
  RN: Leslie Waller

COE, TUCKER
  RN: Donald E. Westlake

COFFIN, GEOFFREY
  RN: Francis Van Wyck Mason

COLEY, ROBERT
  RN: Howard E. Wandrei

COLLIER, HARRY
  RN: Harry Walton

COLLINGWOOD, HARRY
  RN: William J.C. Lancaster

COLLINS, HUNT
  RN: S.A. Lombino

COLLINS, MICHAEL
  RN: Dennis Lynds

COLMORE, G.
  RN: Gertrude Renton

COLSON, BILL
  RN: Verne Athanas

COLT, CLEM
  RN: Nelson Coral Nye

COLTER, ELI
  RN: Mary Elizabeth Counselman

COLVIN, JAMES
  RN: Michael J. Moorcock

COMRADE, ROBERT W.
  RN: Edwy Searles Brooks

CONANT, CHESTER B.
  RN: Chester Cohen

CONN, ALAN
  RN: Allan Connell

CONNINGTON, J.J.
  RN: Alfred Walter Stewart

CONNINGTON, JOHN JERVIS
  RN: Alfred Walter Stewart

CONNOLLY, PAUL
  RN: Thomas Wicker

CONQUEST, JOAN
  RN: Mrs. Leonard Cooke

CONWAY, BOWEN
  RN: John Michel

CONWAY, HUGH
  RN: Frederick John Fargus

CONWAY, RITTER
  RN: Damon Knight

CONWAY, TROY
  RN: Michael Avallone

COOKE, M.E.
  RN: John Creasey

COOMBS, MURDO
  RN: Frederick Clyde Davis

COOPER, JEFFERSON
  RN: Gardner F. Fox

COOVER, WAYNE
  RN: Wolf Detlef Rohr

CORBETT, CHAN
  RN: Nathen Schachner

CORBIN, MICHAEL
  RN: Cleve Cartmill

CORD, BARRY
  RN: Peter B. Germano

CORELLI, MARIE
    RN: Mary Minnie McKay

COREY, HOWARD
    RN: Jack Jardine

CORLEY, ERNEST
    RN: Kenneth Bulmer

CORNING, KYLE
    RN: Erle Stanley Gardner

CORREY, LEE
    RN: G. Harry Stine

CORTIS, DIANA
    RN: Winifred Ashton

CORVO, BARON
    RN: Frederick William Rolfe

CORWIN, CECIL
    RN: Cyril M. Kornbluth

CORY, M.W.M.
    RN: (Matilda) Winifred Graham

COST, MARCH
    RN: Peggy Morrison

COTRION, ANTHONY
    RN: Ernest Lewis Gabrielson

COTTEN, JOHN
    RN: John Russell Fearn

COUPLING, J.J.
    RN: John Pierce

COWPER, RICHARD
    RN: John Middleton Murry

COX, JEAN
    RN: Arthur Jean Cox

CRADDOCK, CHARLES E.
    RN: Mary N. Murfree

CRAIG, A.A.
    RN: Poul Anderson

CRAIG, WEBSTER
    RN: Eric Frank Russell

CRANE, ROBERT
    RN: Bernard Glemser
    RN: Frank Chester Robertson

CRAYON, DIDRICK, JR.
  RN: Kenneth Bruce

CRISPIN, EDMUND
  RN: R.B. Montgomery

CRISTABEL
  RN: Christine Abrahamson

CRITCHIE, ESTIL
  RN: Arthur J. Burkes

CROFT, TAYLOR
  RN: Rupert Croft-Cooke

CROMPTON, RICHMAL
  RN: Richmal C. Lamburn

CROSS, POLTON
  RN: John Russell Fearn

CROSS, STEWART
  RN: Harry Sinclair Drago

CROSS, VICTORIA
  RN: Vivian Cory

CROSSEN, KEN
  RN: Kendall Foster Crossen

CROW, LEVI
  RN: Manly Wade Wellman

CULVER, KATHRYN
  RN: Davis Dresser

CULVER, TIMOTHY J.
  RN: Donald E. Westlake

CUNNINGHAM, E.V.
  RN: Howard Fast

CUNNINGHAM, J. MORGAN
  RN: Donald E. Westlake

CURTIS, WADE
  RN: Jerry Pournelle

DALE, DONALD
  RN: Mary Dale Buckner

DALE, GEORGE E.
  RN: Isaac Asimov

DALEY, HAMLIN
  RN: E. Hoffman Price

D'ALLARD, HUNTER
RN: Willis Todhunter Ballard

DALTON, PRISCILLA
RN: Michael Avallone

DANBERG, NORMAN
RN: Norman Dannenberg

DANBY, FRANK
RN: Mrs. Julia Frankau

DANE, CLEMENCE
RN: Winifred Ashton

DANE, MARK
RN: Michael Avallone

DANIELS, JOHN S.
RN: Wayne D. Overholser

DANIELS, NORMAN
RN: Norman Dannenberg

DANRIT, CAPTAIN
RN: Emile A. Driant

D'ANTIBES, GERMAIN
RN: Georges Simenon

DANVERS, JACK
RN: Camille Auguste Marie Caseleyr

DANZEL, GEORGE
RN: Nelson S. Bond

DARE, ALAN
RN: George Goodchild

DARE, HOWARD
RN: Stuart James Byrne

DARLTON, CLARK
RN: Walter Ernsting

DAVIDSON, HUGH
RN: Edmund Hamilton

DAVIES, WALTER C.
RN: Cyril M. Kornbluth

DAVIOT, GORDON
RN: Elizabeth MacIntosh

DAVIS, DON
RN: Davis Dresser

DAWSON, PETER
  RN: Jonathan H. Glidden

DAY, MAX
  RN: Bruce Cassiday

De ACTON, EUGENIA
  RN: Alethea Lewis

DEAN, PAUL
  RN: Gardner F. Fox

DEANE, NORMAN
  RN: John Creasey

DEARBORN, LAURA
  RN: Nina Picton

De COSTA, HENRY
  RN: Frederik Pohl

DEE, ROGER
  RN: Roger D. Aycock

DEEPING, WARWICK
  RN: George Warwick Deeping

DEGEN, VON
  RN: Ann C. Rabe

de GRAEFF, W.B.
  RN: Groff Conklin

DEHAN, RICHARD
  RN: Clotilde Graves

DELL, DUDLEY
  RN: H.L. Gold

Del MARTIA, ASTRON
  RN: John Russell Fearn

DELORME, CHARLES
  RN: Charles Rumball

DEMING, KIRK
  RN: Harry Sinclair Drago

DENHOLM, MARK
  RN: John Russell Fearn

DENNIS, BRUCE
  RN: David Wright O'Brien

DENTINGER, STEPHEN
  RN: Edward D. Hoch

DENVER, DRAKE C.
  RN: Nelson Coral Nye

De PRE, JEAN-ANNE
  RN: Michael Avallone

DERSONNE, JACQUES
  RN: Georges Simenon

de ST. LEON, COUNT REGINALD
  RN: Edward Du Bois

D'ESME, JEAN
  RN: Jean D'Esmenard

DEVEREUX, ROY
  RN: Margaret R. Pember-Devereux

deWREDER, PAUL
  RN: John W. Hemming

DEXTER, MARTIN
  RN: Frederick Faust

DEXTER, PETER
  RN: Richard S. Shaver

DEXTER, WILLIAM
  RN: William Thomas Pritchard

DICK, R.A.
  RN: Josephine A. Leslie

DICKBERRY, F.
  RN: F. Blaze De Bury

DICKSON, CARR
  RN: John Dickson Carr

DICKSON, CARTER
  RN: John Dickson Carr

DINESEN, ISAK
  RN: Baroness Karen Blixen

DIOSCORIDES, DR.
  RN: Peter Harting

D'ISLEY, GEORGES
  RN: Georges Simenon

DIVINE, DAVID
  RN: Arthur Durham Divine

DIVINE, DOMINICK
  RN: David Macdonald Divine

ЭCHERTY, JAMES
  RN: Rene Raymond

DODD, DOUGLAS
  RN: John Russell Fearn

DOE, JOHN
  RN: Tiffany Ellsworth Thayer

DOGBOLT, BARNABY
  RN: Henry Silvette

DONOVAN, DICK
  RN: E.P. Joyce Muddock

DORSAGE, JEAN
  RN: Georges Simenon

DORSAN, LUC
  RN: Georges Simenon

DORSET, ST. JOHN
  RN: Hugh J. Belfour

DOSSAGE, JEAN
  RN: Georges Simenon

DOUGLAS, LEONARD
  RN: Ray Bradbury

DOUGLAS, THEO
  RN: Mrs. H.D. Everett

DOYLE, JOHN
  RN: Robert Graves

DRAYNE, GEORGE
  RN: Johnstone McCulley

DREW, SHERIDAN
  RN: John Russell Fearn

DREXEL, JAY B.
  RN: Jerome Bixby

DUANE, ANDREW
  RN: Robert Edward Briney

DUANE, TOBY
  RN: W. Paul Ganley

DUCHESS, THE
  RN: Margaret W. Hungerford

DUNN, GERTRUDE C.
  RN: Gertrude Weaver

DUNSTAN, ANDREW
  RN: A. Bertram Chandler

DuPERRY, JEAN
  RN: Georges Simenon

DURHAM, DAVID
  RN: Roy Vickers

DYE, CHARLES
  RN: Katherine MacLean (See note under her name in
    Section I.)

EAGLE, SOLOMON
  RN: Sir John Collings Squire

EARLE, W.J.
  RN: Luis Philip Senarens

EDMUNDS, PAUL
  RN: Henry Kuttner

EDSON, GEORGE ALDEN
  RN: Paul Ernst

EDWARDS, CHARMAN
  RN: Frederick A. Edwards

EDWARDS, GAWAIN
  RN: Edward Pendray

EDWARDS, HAMM
  RN: Mrs. E. Everett Evans

EDWARDS, JOHN MILTON
  RN: William Wallace Cook

EGBERT, H.M.
  RN: Victor Emmanuel Rousseau

EGERTON, GEORGE
  RN: Mary C. Bright

EIRE, ROBERT L.
  RN: Robert L. Fish

ELDON, CLEO
  RN: Don Wilcox

ELEVE
  RN: Mrs. H.M. Stowe

ELIOT, E.C.
  RN: R.A. Martin

ELLERMAN, GENE
  RN: Basil Wells

ELLIOTT, WILLIAM
  RN: Ray Bradbury

ELLSWORTH, ELMER, JR.
  RN: Tiffany Ellsworth Thayer

ELRON
  RN: L. Ron Hubbard

ELSTAR, DON
  RN: Raymond Z. Gallun

ELSTON, MAX
  RN: John Russell Fearn

ELTON, JOHN
  RN: John Marsh

EMSH
  RN: Edmund Alexander Emshwiller

ENGLISH, CHARLES
  RN: Charles Alexander Nuetzel

ERICKSON, WALTER
  RN: Howard Fast

ERMAN, JACQUES DeFOREST
  RN: Forrest J. Ackerman

ERMAYNE, LAURAJEAN
  RN: Forrest J. Ackerman

ERMINE, WILL
  RN: Harry Sinclair Drago

ERVIN, PATRICK
  RN: Robert E. Howard

ESTERBROOK, TOM
  RN: L. Ron Hubbard

ESTEVAN, JOHN
  RN: Samuel Shellabarger

ETTRICK SHEPHERD, THE
  RN: James Hogg

EUSTACE, ROBERT
  RN: Eustace R. Barton

EVAN, EVIN
  RN: Frederick Faust

EVANS, EVAN
  RN: Frederick Faust

EVANS, IAN
  RN: Angus Wells

EWING, FREDERICK R.
  RN: Theodore Sturgeon

F.O.O.
  RN: Cecil John Charles Street

FAIR, A.A.
  RN: Erle Stanley Gardner

FAIRLESS, MICHAEL
  RN: Margaret Barber

FALCONER, KENNETH
  RN: Cyril M. Kornbluth

FALCONER, LANCE
  RN: Mary E. Hawker

FALLADA, HANS
  RN: Rudolf Ditzen

FANE, BRON
  RN: Robert Lionel Fanthorpe

FARLEY, RALPH MILNE
  RN: Roger Sherman Hoar

FARNESWORTH, DUNCAN
  RN: David Wright O'Brien

FARNINGHAM, MARIANNE
  RN: Mary Hearn

FARRELL, JOHN WADE
  RN: John D. MacDonald

FARRERE, CLAUDE
  RN: Charles Bargone

FENIMORE, W.
  RN: A. Merritt

FIELD, FRANK CHESTER
  RN: Frank Chester Robertson

FIELD, GANS T.
  RN: Manly Wade Wellman

FIELDING, HOWARD
  RN: Charles Hooke

FIGHTON, GEORGE Z.
  RN: Winteler De Weindeck, U.M.C.

IRTH, WESLEY
  RN: John Russell Fearn

FISHER, CLAY
  RN: William Henry Allen

FISKE, TARLETON
  RN: Robert Bloch

FITT, MARY
  RN: Kathleen Freeman

FITZGERALD, CAPT. HUGH
  RN: L. Frank Baum

FITZGERALD, WILLIAM
  RN: William Fitzgerald Jenkins

FLAGG, FRANCIS
  RN: George Henry Weiss

FLAMMARION, CAMILLE
  RN: Nicolas Camille Flammarion

FLAMMENBURG, LORENZ
  RN: Karl F. Kahlert

FLANDERS, JOHN
  RN: Raymond De Kremer

FLEMING, STUART
  RN: Damon Knight

FLETCHER, GEORGE U.
  RN: Fletcher Pratt

FLORIANI, GIULIO
  RN: Aubrey Beardsley

FOOL, TOM
  RN: Robert Graves

FORD, ELBUR
  RN: Eleanor Burford Hibbert

FORD, LESLIE
  RN: Zenith Jones Brown

FORD, LEWIS B.
  RN: Lewis Byford Patten

FORREST, FELIX C.
  RN: Paul Linebarger

FORTUNE, DION
  RN: Violet Mary Firth

FOSCHTER, ALBERT
  RN: Aubrey Beardsley

FOSSE, HAROLD C.
  RN: H.L. Gold

FOSTER, RICHARD
  RN: Kendall Foster Crossen

FOWLER, SYDNEY
  RN: Sydney Fowler Wright

FRANCE, ANATOLE
  RN: Jacques Anatole Thibeault

FRANCHEZZO
  RN: A. Farnese

FRANKLIN, EDGAR
  RN: Albert Stearns

FRANKLIN, JAY
  RN: John Franklin Carter

FRANKLIN, PAUL
  RN: Bryce Walton

FRAZER, ROBERT CAINE
  RN: John Creasey

FREDERICK, JOHN
  RN: Frederick Faust

FREDERICKS, ARNOLD
  RN: Frederick Arnold Kummer

FREEMAN, R. AUSTIN
  RN: Richard Austin Freeman

FRENCH, PAUL
  RN: Isaac Asimov

FREYER, ERICK
  RN: Frederick Shroyer

FREYER, FREDERICK
  RN: William S. Ballinger

FRIKELL, SAMRI
  RN: H. Bedford Jones

FROME, DAVID
  RN: Zenith Jones Brown

FROST, FREDERICK
  RN: Frederick Faust

FRYERS, AUSTIN
  RN: William Clery

FUGITIVE, A
  RN: Edward D. Coxe

FUQUA, ROBERT
  RN: Joe W. Tillotson

FUREY, MICHAEL
  RN: Arthur Salsfield Ward

FURTH, CARLTON
  RN: Joe Gibson

FUZE
  RN: Robert Graves

GABRIEL, JOHN
  RN: Ernest Lewis Gabrielson

GAGE, WILSON
  RN: Mary Quintard Steele

GALAXAN, SOL
  RN: Alfred Coppel

GANPAT
  RN: Martin L. Gompertz

GARDENER, HARRY J.
  RN: E. Everett Evans

GARDENER, NOEL
  RN: Henry Kuttner

GARETT, RANDALL
  RN: Robert Silverberg

GARFIELD, FRANCES
  RN: Mrs. Manly Wade Wellman

GARLAND, LUKE
  RN: John Harvey Whitson

GARRON, ROBERT A.
  RN: Howard E. Wandrei

GASHBACK, GRENO
  RN: Hugo Gernsback

GASKELL, JANE
  RN: Jane Lynch

GAWSWORTH, JOHN
  RN: Terrance Ian Fytton Armstrong

GAYLORD, TIMEUS
  RN: Clark Ashton Smith

GENONE, HUDOR
  RN: William James Roe

GEORGE, VERNON
  RN: George S.G. Vernon

GEORGES, GEORGES MARTIN
  RN: Georges Simenon

GERAHTY, DIGBY GEORGE
  RN: Robert Standish

GERIS, TOM IRWIN
  RN: Mort Weisinger

GERRARE, WIRT
  RN: William O. Greener

GIBBS, LEWIS
  RN: Joseph Walter Cove

GILES, GORDON A.
  RN: Otto Binder

GILHOOLEY, LORD
  RN: Frederick H. Seymour

GILL, PATRICK
  RN: John Creasey

GILMAN, ROBERT CHAM
  RN: Alfred Coppel

GLAMIS, WALTER
  RN: Nathen Schachner

GODFREY, HALL
  RN: Charlotte O. Eccles

GOLDTHWAITE, JAMES A.
  RN: Francis James

GOODWIN, JOHN
  RN: Sidney F. Gowing

GORDON, DAVID
  RN: Randall Garrett

GORDON, DONALD
  RN: Donald Gordon Payne

GORDON, MILLARD VERNE
  RN: Don Wollheim

GORDON, REX
  RN: Stanley Bennett Hough

GOULD, ARTHUR LEE
  RN: Arthur S.G. Lee

GOULD, STEPHEN
  RN: Stephen Gould Fisher

GRAHAM, HARVEY
  RN: Isaac H. Flack

GRAHAM, WILLIAM
  RN: Arthur Louis Joquel II

GRAHAME, FELIX
  RN: Fred Brown

GRAHAME, HOWARD
  RN: Howard E. Wandrei

GRAHAME, WINIFRED
  RN: Matilda W. Cory

GRANT, AMBROSE
  RN: Rene Raymond

GRANT, DON
  RN: Donald Frank Glut

GRANTLAND, KEITH
  RN: Charles Nutt

GRAY, CHARLES
  RN: E.C. Tubb

GRAY, JONATHAN
  RN: Herbert Adams

GRAY, RUSSELL
  RN: Bruno Fischer

GREEN, CHARLES M.
  RN: Erle Stanley Gardner

GREGOR, LEE
  RN: Milton Rothman

GREGORY, HARRY
  RN: Theodore Mark Gottfried

GREGORY, STEPHEN
  RN: Don Pendleton

GRENDON, STEPHEN
  RN: August Derleth

GRIFF, ALAN
  RN: William Donald Suddaby

GRINNELL, DAVID
  RN: Don Wollheim

GRIP
  RN: Edgar L. Welch

GRUELLE, JOHNNY
  RN: John Barton

GUERNSEY, H.W.
  RN: Howard E. Wandrei

GUILLAUME, ROBERT
  RN: Robert W. Sneddon

GULLIVER, LEMUEL
  RN: Jonathan Swift

GUNN, JAMES A.
  RN: James E. Gunn

GUTHRIE, ALAN
  RN: E.C. Tubb

GWYNNE, PAUL
  RN: Ernest Slater

HABERGOOK, GUS N.
  RN: Hugo Gernsback

HADLEY, FRANKLIN
  RN: Russ Winterbotham

HAGGARD, WILLIAM
  RN: Richard Clayton

HALE, RUSS
  RN: William Bogart

HALL, ADAM
  RN: Elleston Trevor

HALL, CAMERON
  RN: Lester del Rey

HALL, JAMES
  RN: Henry Kuttner

HALL, OWEN
  RN: James Davis

HALLAM, ATLANTIS
  RN: Samuel Behoni

HALLIDAY, BRETT
  RN: Davis Dresser

HALLIDAY, MICHAEL
  RN: John Creasey

HALLUS, TAK
  RN: Stephen Robinett

HAMILTON, CLIVE
  RN: C.S. Lewis

HAMILTON, ERNEST
  RN: Josephine Judith Grossman

HAMM, T.D.
  RN: Mrs. E. Everett Evans

HAMMOND, KEITH
  RN: Henry Kuttner

HARD, FRANCIS
  RN: Farnesworth Wright

HARDY, ADAM
  RN: Kenneth H. Bulmer

HARE, ROBERT
  RN: Robert H. Hutchinson

HARLEY, JOHN
  RN: John Marsh

HARMON, H.H.
  RN: Robert Moore Williams

HARPER, OLIVE
  RN: Helen D'Apery

HARRISON, BRUCE
  RN: Edgar Pangborn

HARRISON, WHIT
  RN: Harry Whittington

HART, ELLIS
  RN: Harlan Ellison

HARTLEY, CHRISTINE
  RN: C(hristine) C(ampbell) Thomson

HARTLEY, MALCOLM
  RN: John Russell Fearn

HASTING, CONSUL
  RN: Alfred Galpin

HASTINGS, HARRINGTON
  RN: John Marsh

HASTWA, A.
  RN: H.S.W. Chibbett

HATHAWAY, LOUIS
  RN: Maria Metlova

HAY, IAN
  RN: John Hay Beith

HAYNES, JOHN ROBERT
  RN: Philip Wilding

HAZEL, WILLIAM
  RN: Margaret St. Clair

HAZELTINE, HORACE
  RN: Charles Stokes Wayne

HAZELTON, CAPT./COL.
  RN: John Harvey Whitson

HEARD, GERALD
  RN: Henry Fitzgerald Heard

HEARD, H.F.
  RN: Henry Fitzgerald Heard

HELLER, FRANK
  RN: Martin G. Serner

HELVICK, JAMES
  RN: Claud Cockburn

HENRY, EDGAR
  RN: Albion W. Tourgee

HENRY, MARION
  RN: Lester del Rey

HENRY, ROBERT
  RN: John D. MacDonald

HENRY, WILL
  RN: William Henry Allen

HERITAGE, MARTIN
  RN: Sydney Horler

HERMES
  RN: Benjamin Lumley

HERRICK, THORNECLIFFE
  RN: Jerome Bixby

HERTZ-GARDEN, T.
  RN: Mrs. De Mattos

HERWELL, ROGER
  RN: John Boardman

HEXT, HARRINGTON
  RN: Eden Phillpots

HICKEY, H.B.
  RN: Herb Livingston

HIGHLAND, DORA
  RN: Michael Avallone

HILL, H. HAVERSTOCK
  RN: James Morgan Walsh

HILL, HEADON
  RN: Francis Grainger

HILL, KING
  RN: Frank Chester Robertson

HINDEN, NATHEN
  RN: Robert Bloch

HODGE, SHIRBY T.
  RN: Roger S. Tracy

HOGARTH, CHARLES
  RN: John Creasey

HOLBERG, LEWIS
  RN: Baron Von Ludwig Lewis

HOLLAND, CLIVE
  RN: Charles J. Hankinson

HOLLAND, KATRIN
  RN: Heidi Huberta Freybe

HOLLAND, KEL
  RN: Harry Whittington

HOLLIS, H.H.
  RN: Ben C. Ramey

HOLLY, J. HUNTER
  RN: Joan C. Holly

HOLMES, A.R.
  RN: Harry Bates

HOLMES, H.H.
  RN: William Anthony Parker White

HOLT, C.G.
  RN: John Russell Fearn

HOLT, CONRAD
  RN: John Russell Fearn

HOLT, TEX
  RN: Archie L. Joscelyn

HOLT, VICTORIA
  RN: Eleanor Burford Hibbert

HOLTON, LEONARD
  RN: Leonard Patrick O'Connor Wibberley

HOMES, GEOFFREY
  RN: Daniel Mainwaring

HOPE, ANTHONY
  RN: Anthony Hope Hawkins

HOPE, BRIAN
  RN: John Creasey

HOPLEY, GEORGE
  RN: Cornell Woolrich

HOUGHTON, CLAUDE
  RN: Claude Houghton Oldfield

HOVEN, ERNIEST
  RN: Fanny Hooker

HOVORRE, M. AUBURRE
  RN: Albert Waldo Howard

HOWARD, KEBLE
  RN: John Keble Bell

HOWARD, PATRICK
  RN: Robert E. Howard

HOWARD, POLICE CAPTAIN
  RN: Luis Philip Senarens

HOWES, JANE
  RN: Wilmar H. Shiras

HUDSON, JEFFREY
  RN: J. Michael Crichton

HUGHES, COLIN
  RN: John Creasey

HUGI, MORRIS J.
  (See Eric Frank Russell, Section I.)

HUNT, GILL
  RN: E.C. Tubb

HUNT, HARRISON
  RN: Willis Todhunter Ballard

HUNT, KYLE
  RN: John Creasey

HUNTER, CLINGHAM, M.D.
  RN: William T. Adams

HUNTER, E. WALDO
  RN: Theodore Sturgeon

HUNTER, EVAN
  RN: S.A. Lombino

HUNTER, HALL
  RN: Eddison Marshall

HUNTER, JOHN
  RN: Willis Todhunter Ballard

HUSSINGTREE, MARTIN
  RN: Oliver Baldwin

ILES, FRANCIS
  RN: Anthony Berkeley Cox

INGOLDSBY, THOMAS
  RN: Richard Henry Barham

INNES, MICHAEL
  RN: John Innes Mackintosh Stewart

IRELAND, M.J.
  RN: Joslyn Maxwell

IRELAND, MICHAEL
  RN: Darrell Figgis

IRISH, WILLIAM
  RN: Cornell Woolrich

IRVING, COMPTON
  RN: John L.J. Carter

IRWIN, MARGARET
  RN: Mrs. John Robert Monsell

J.T.
  RN: Eric Temple Bell

JACKSON, STEPHEN
  RN: John Stevenson

JAMES, EDWIN
  RN: James Gunn

JAMES, HENRY (c. 1929 pulps)
  RN: L.C. Kellenberger

JAMES, PHILIP
  RN: Lester del Rey

JAMESON, STORM
  RN: Margaret Storm Chapman

JANIFER, LAURENCE M.
  (See Larry M. Harris, Section I.)

JANS, EMERSON
  RN: Jerome Bixby

JANVIER, PAUL
  RN: Algerdas Jonas Budrys

JASON, JOHNNY
  RN: Donald Frank Glut

JEROME, OWEN FOX
  RN: Oscar J. Friend

JESSEL, JOHN
  RN: Stanley G. Weinbaum

JOHN, JASPER
  RN: Rosalie Muspratt

JOHNHETT
  RN: John Hettinger

JOHNSON, CROCKETT
  RN: David Johnson Leisk

JOHNSTONE, TED
  RN: David McDaniel

JONES, FRANK
  RN: John Russell Fearn

JONES, JOHN J.
  RN: H.P. Lovecraft

JONQUIL
  RN: J.L. Collins

KAEMPFERT, WADE
  RN: Lester del Rey

KAINS, JOSEPHINE
  RN: Ron Goulart

KARISHKA, PAUL
  RN: Davidson Patterson Hatch

KARLOFF, BORIS
  RN: William Henry Pratt

KAY, IAN
  RN: John Hay Beith

KAYE, MARX
  RN: Stuart James Byrne

KAYNE, MARVIN
  RN: John Russell Fearn

KEITH, COLIN
  RN: Malcom Jameson

KEITH, MICHAEL
  RN: L. Ron Hubbard

KELL, JOSEPH
  RN: John Anthony Burgess Wilson

KELLINO, PAMELA
  RN: Pamela Mason

KELLOW, KATHLEEN
  RN: Eleanor Burford Hibbert

KENDALL, JOHN
  RN: Margaret M. Brash

KENDRAKE, CARLETON
  RN: Erle Stanley Gardner

KENDRICKS, JAMES
  RN: Gardner F. Fox

KENNEDY, PHILIP
  RN: Harold Hersey

KENNY, CHARLES J.
  RN: Erle Stanley Gardner

KENT, MALLORY
  RN: Robert W. Lowndes

KENT, PHILIP
  RN: Kenneth Bulmer

KENTON, BERNARD J.
  Jerome Siegel

KENYON, ROBERT O.
  RN: Henry Kuttner

KEPAC, COIL
  RN: Forrest J. Ackerman

KERBY, SUSAN ALICE
  RN: Elizabeth J. Burton

KERLAY, ALLIS
  RN: Forrest J. Ackerman

KERN, GREGORY
  RN: E.C. Tubb

KEYES, DURHAM
  RN: Durham Keith Garton

KIMBALL, CONRAD
  RN: Wayne Rogers

KING, RAY
  RN: Ray Cummings

KINGSMILL, HUGH
  RN: Hugh K. Lunn

KINGSTON, JOHN
  RN: Keith Roberts

KIPPAX, JOHN
  RN: John Hynam

KIPROY, CHARLES
  RN: Harold Hersey

KIRK, LAURENCE
  RN: Eric Andrew Simson

KLIMARIS, J.S.
  RN: Walter Kubilius

KNOX, CALVIN M.
  RN: Robert Silverberg

KNOX, LISBETH
  RN: Rose Elizabeth Knox Ward

KUMARA, SANANDANA
  RN: Roger P. Graham

KUPPORD, SKELTON
  RN: J. Adams

KURZ, ARTHUR R.
  RN: Thomas Nicholas Scortia

KYLE, SEFTON
  RN: Roy Vickers

LaFARGUE, PHILIP
  RN: Joseph Henry Philpot

LAFAYETTE, RENE
  RN: L. Ron Hubbard

LAING, PATRICK
  RN: Amelia Reynolds Long

LAMBERT, CHRISTINE
  RN: Heidi Huberta Freybe

LAMBERT, S.H.
  RN: Stephen Southwold

LAMONT, DUNCAN
  RN: E.C. Tubb

LANCING, GEORGE
  RN: Bluebell M. Hunter

LANE, ARTHUR
  RN: F. Orlin Tremaine

LANE, GRANT
  RN: William Bogart
  RN: Stephen Gould Fisher

LANE, JOHN
  RN: John D. MacDonald

LANE, TEMPLE
  RN: Mary Isabel Leslie

LANG, KING
  RN: John Russell Fearn
  RN: E.C. Tubb
  (The Lang PN was used separately by both Fearn & Tubb.)

LANGART, DARREL T.
  RN: Randall Garrett

LANGE, JOHN
  RN: J. Michael Crichton

LARROVITCH
  RN: Harold Hersey

LATHAM, PHILIP
  RN: Robert S. Richardson

LAURIE, A.
  RN: Paschal Grousset

LAW-ABIDING REVOLUTIONIST, A
  RN: Bert J. Wellman

LAWRENCE
  RN: Lawrence Sterne Stevens

LAWRENCE, MARGERY
  RN: Mrs. A.E. Towle

LAWSON, W.B.
  RN: William Wallace Cook

LAWTON, DENNIS
  RN: Frederick Faust

LeCOQ, MONSIEUR
  RN: Georges Simenon

LEE, MATT
  RN: Sam Merwin, Jr.

LEE, VERNON
  RN: Violet Paget

LEE, WILLIAM
  RN: William S. Burroughs

LEGIONNAIRE 14830
  RN: L. Ron Hubbard

LEIGH, JOHANNA
  RN: Dorothy L(eigh) Sayers

LEIGHTON, LEE
  RN: Wayne D. Overholser

LEINSTER, MURRAY
  RN: William Fitzgerald Jenkins

LEITCH, LAVINIA
  RN: Lavinia Hynd

LEMKE, HENRY E.
  RN: Richard Tooker

LeMOYNE, ROY
  RN: Harold Hersey

LENNOX, JOHN
  RN: Alfred Bester

LEONHART, RAPHAEL W.
  RN: Peter Wybraniec

LEPPOC, DERFLA
  RN: Alfred Coppel

LeSIEG, THEO
  RN: Theodore Seuss Geisel

LESLIE, O.H.
  RN: Henry Slesar

LESLIE, WILLIAM
  RN: Violet Perkins

LESSER, DERWIN
  RN: Charles D. Hornig

LEWIS, D.B.
  RN: Jerome Bixby

LIN, FRANK
  RN: Gertrude Atherton

LITTLEWIT, HUMPHREY
  RN: H.P. Lovecraft

LLOYD, CHARLES
  RN: Charles Lloyd Birkin

LLOYD, HERBERT
  RN: John Russell Fearn

LOCKHARD, LEONARD
  RN: Theodore L. Thomas

LOGAN, WILLIAM
  RN: Laurence M. Janifer

LOMAX, BLISS
  RN: Henry Sinclair Drago

LONG, WESLEY
  RN: George O. Smith

LORAC, E.C.R.
  RN: Edith Caroline Rivett

LORRAINE, ALDEN
  RN: Forrest J. Ackerman

LOVEHILL, C.B.
  RN: Charles Nutt

LOXMITH, JOHN
  RN: John Brunner

LURGAN, LESTER
  RN: Mabel W. Knowles

LUSKA, SIDNEY
  RN: Henry Harland

LYMINGTON, JOHN
  RN: John Newton Chance

LYON, LYMAN R.
  RN: L. Sprague De Camp

LYONS, MARCUS
  RN: James Blish

LYS, CHRISTIAN
  RN: Percy Brebnor

MacAPP, C.C.
  RN: Carroll M. Capps

MacARTHUR, BURKE
  RN: Arthur J. Burkes

McBAIN, ED
  RN: S.A. Lombino

McCANN, ARTHUR
  RN: John W. Campbell, Jr.

McCORMICK, BROOKS
  RN: William T. Adams

McCREADY, JACK
  RN: Talmadge Powell

MacCREIGH, JAMES
  RN: Frederik Pohl

McCRIB, THEOPHILUS
  RN: Henry B. Lee

McCULLOCH, JOHN TYLER
  RN: Edgar Rice Burroughs

MacDONALD, ANSON
  RN: Robert A. Heinlein

MACDONALD, JOHN
  RN: Kenneth Millar

MACDONALD, JOHN ROSS
  RN: Kenneth Millar

MACDONALD, ROSS
  RN: Kenneth Millar

McDOW, GERALD
  RN: Thomas Nicholas Scortia

MacDUFF, ANDREW
  RN: Horace B. Fyfe

McFARLAND, STEPHEN
  RN: John Keir Cross

McGOWAN, INEZ
  RN: Roger P. Graham

MacGREGOR, MARY
  RN: Malcom Jameson

MacINTOSH, G.T.
  RN: James Murdock MacGregor

McKENNA, EVELYN
  RN: Archie L. Joscelyn

McKENZIE, RAY
  RN: Robert Silverberg

MacLEOD, FIONA
  RN: William Sharp

McMAHON, PAT
  RN: Edward D. Hoch

MacNEIL, NEIL
  RN: Willis Todhunter Ballard

McNUTT, CHARLES
  RN: Charles Nutt

MacPATTERSON, F.
  RN: Walter Ernsting

MADDOCK, LARRY
  RN: Jack Jardine

MADDOCK, STEPHEN
  RN: James Morgen Walsh

MADDOX, CARL
  RN: E.C. Tubb

MAEPEN, K.H.
  RN: Henry Kuttner

MAGRISKA, COUNTESS HELENE
  RN: Enid F. Brockies

MAGROON, VICTOR
  RN: John Russell Fearn

MAINE, CHARLES ERIC
  RN: David McIlwaine

MAJORS, SIMON
  RN: Gardner F. Fox

MALCOLM, DAN
  RN: Robert Silverberg

MALET, LUCAS
  RN: Mary S. Harrison

MALET, ORIEL
  RN: Auriel R. Vaughan

MALLIK, B.K.
  RN: Robert Graves

MANASCO, NORMAN
  RN: Wyman Guin

MANN, ABEL
  RN: John Creasey

MANN, JACK
  RN: E. Charles Vivien

MANNING, DAVID
  RN: Frederick Faust

MAN OF THE PEOPLE, A
  RN: W. Thomson

MANTON, PETER
  RN: John Creasey

MARAS, KARL
  RN: Kenneth Bulmer

MARINER, SCOTT
  RN: Cyril M. Kornbluth

MARK, TED
  RN: Theodore Mark Gottfried

MARKHAM, ROBERT
  RN: Kingsley Amis

MARLOWE, LOUIS
  RN: Louis U. Wilkinson

MARLOWE, STEPHEN
  RN: Milton Lesser

MARLOWE, WEBB
  RN: Francis McComas

MARRIC, J.J.
  RN: John Creasey

MARSDEN, ANTHONY
  RN: Graham Sutton

MARSHALL, JAMES VANCE
  RN: Donald Gordon Payne

MARSHALL, RAYMOND
  RN: Rene Raymond

MARSTEN, RICHARD
  RN: S.A. Lombino

MARTENS, PAUL
  RN: Stephen Southwold

MARTIN, KEN
  RN: L. Ron Hubbard

MARTIN, RICHARD
  RN: John Creasey

MARTIN, SAM
  RN: Sam Moskowitz

MARTIN, WEBBER
  RN: Robert Silverberg

MARTYN, PHILLIP
  RN: E.C. Tubb

MARVELL, ANDREW
  RN: Howell Davies

MASON, FRANK W.
  RN: F. Van Wyck Mason

MASON, TALLY
  RN: August Derleth

MASSEY, JAMES
  RN: Simon Tyssot De Patot

MATTHEWS, KEVIN
  RN: Gardner F. Fox

MAURICE, MICHAEL
  RN: Conrad A. Skinner

MAVITY, HUBERT
  RN: Nelson S. Bond

MAY, JONATHAN
  RN: Laurence James

MAYNWARING, ARCHIBALD
  RN: H.P. Lovecraft

MAYO, JIM
  RN: Louis L'Amour

MAYON, MARIAN & FRANKLIN
  RN: Frank Rosewater

MEADE, L.T.
  RN: Elizabeth Thomasina Meade Smith

MEREDITH, HAL
  RN: Harry Blyth

MEREDITH, OWEN
  RN: Edward Robert Bulwer-Lytton

MERLIN, ARTHUR
  RN: James Blish

MERRILL, JUDITH
  RN: Josephine Judith Grossman

MERRILL, P.J.
  RN: Holly Roth

MERRIMAN, ALEX
  RN: Robert Silverberg

MERRITT, KATARIN MARKOV
  RN: Forrest J. Ackerman

MERRIWELL, FRANK
  RN: John Harvey Whitson

MICHAELS, BARBARA
  RN: Barbara Mertz

MICHAELS, STEVE
  RN: Michael Avallone

MIKALOWITCH, NIKOLAI
  RN: Nicholas Michels

MILES
  RN: Stephen Southwold

MILLER, BENJ.
  RN: Noel Loomis

MILLER, FRANK
  RN: Noel Loomis

MILLER, JOHN
  RN: Joseph Samachson

MITCHELL, GENE
  RN: H.O. Hoadley

MONETT, LIREVE
  RN: Everil Worrell

MONIG, CHRISTOPHER
  RN: Kendall Foster Crossen

MONROE, LYLE
  RN: Robert A. Heinlein

MOORE, ROBERT
  RN: Robert Moore Williams

MORDAUNT, ELINOR
  RN: Evelyn M. Mordaunt

MORE, ANTHONY
  RN: Edwin M. Clinton

MOREL, DIGHTON
  RN: Kenneth Lewis Warner

MORELAND, PETER HENRY
  RN: Frederick Faust

MORELL, CHARLES
  RN: James Ridley

MORESBY, LOUIS
  RN: Lily Adams Beck

MORETON, ANTHONY
  RN: John Creasey

MORGAN, SCOTT
  RN: Henry Kuttner

MORISON, FRANK
  RN: Albert Ross

MORLEY, BRIAN
  RN: Marian Zimmer Bradley

MORLEY, WILFRED OWEN
  RN: Robert W. Lowndes

MOROJO
  RN: Myrtle R. Douglas

MORRISON, RICHARD
  RN: Robert W. Lowndes

MORRISON, VICTOR
  RN: Donald Frank Glut

MORRISON, WILLIAM
  RN: Joseph Samachson

MUDGETT, HERMAN W.
  RN: William Anthony Parker White

MUIR, JAMES A.
  RN: Angus Wells

MUNRO, DUNCAN H.
  RN: Eric Frank Russell

MURPHY, JASPER DENNIS
  RN: Charles Maturin

MURRY, COLIN
  RN: John Middleton Murry

MYERS, HARRIET KATHRYN
  RN: Harry Whittington

MYSELF & ANOTHER
  RN: Edward A. Caswell

NADER, SEENA
  RN: Forrest J. Ackerman

na GOPALEEN, MYLES
  RN: Brian O Nuallain

NATHAN, DANIEL
  RN: Frederick Dannay

NEAL, GAVIN
  RN: E.C. Tubb

NEAL, HARRY
  RN: Jerome Bixby

NEMO, OMEN
  RN: Warren S. Rehm

NETTERFIELD, LUKE
  RN: Standish O'Grady

NETTERVILLE, LUKE
  RN: Standish O'Grady

NETZEN, KLAUS
  RN: Laurence James

NEWMAN, A.
  RN: Herbert M. Pim

NEWMAN, ROBERT
  RN: Roger Howard Norton

NICHOLS, SCOTT
  RN: Thomas Nicholson Scortia

NICHOLSON, JOHN
  RN: Norman H. Parcell

NIHIL
  RN: P. Schuyler Miller

NILE, DOROTHEA
  RN: Michael Avallone

NOEL, L.
  RN: Leonard N. Barker

NOLAN, CHRISTOPHER
  RN: Laurence James

NONAME
  RN: Luis Philip Senarens

NOONE, EDWINA
  RN: Michael Avallone

NORBERT, W.
  RN: Norbert Wiener

NORFOLK, WILLIAM
  RN: Philip José Farmer

NORMAN, JOHN
  RN: John Frederick Lange

NORMYX
  RN: Norman Douglas

NORTH, ANDREW
  RN: Alice Mary Norton

NORTH, ERIC
  RN: Bernard Cronin

NORTHEN, LESLIE
  RN: Frank Belknap Long

NORTON, ANDRE
  RN: Alice Mary Norton

NOSTRADAMUS, MERLIN
  RN: Frances P. Cobbe

NOTTE, ASTRID
  RN: Forrest J. Ackerman

NUVERBIS
  RN: Dillon Jordan Spotswood

O'BRIEN, E.G.
  RN: Arthur C. Clarke

O'BRIEN, FLANN
  RN: Brian O Nuallain

O'CONNOR, PATRICK
  RN: Leonard Patrick O'Connor Wibberley

O'DONNELL, K.M.
  RN: Barry Malzberg

O'DONNEVAN, FINN
  RN: Robert Sheckley

OGILVY, GAVIN
  RN: Sir James M. Barrie

O'GRADY, ROHAN
  RN: June O'Grady Skinner

O'HARA, KENNETH
  RN: Bryce Walton

O'HARA, SCOTT
  RN: John D. MacDonald

OLD STAGER
  RN. William T. Adams

OLE LUKE-OIE
  RN: Sir Ernest Dunlop Swinton

OLSEN, BOB
  RN: Alfred John Olsen, Jr.

O'MALLEY, FRANK
  RN: Frank O'Rourke

ONIONS, OLIVER
  RN: George Oliver

O NOLAN, BRIAN
  RN: Brian O Nuallain

OPTIC, OLIVER
  RN: William T. Adams

ORCHARDS, THEODORE
  RN: Charles (Stewart) Palmer

ORTH, BENNINGTON
  RN: Roger Sherman Hoar

ORWELL, GEORGE
  RN: Eric Arthur Blair

OSBORNE, DAVID
  RN: Robert Silverberg

OSBORNE, GEORGE
  RN: Robert Silverberg

OTIS, JAMES
  RN: Otis James Kaler

OVERTON, MAX
  RN: Don Wilcox

OWEN, ALBERT
  RN: Harold Hersey

OWEN, DEAN
  RN: Dudley Dean McGaughy

OWEN, FRANK
  RN: Roswell Williams

OWEN, HUGH
  RN: Frederick Faust

OWEN, JOHN PICKARD
  RN: Samuel Butler

OWEN, WILLIAM BICKERSTETH
  RN: Samuel Butler

OXENHAM, JOHN
  RN: William A. Dunkerley

PAGE, MARCO
  RN: Harry Kurnitz

PAGET-LOWE, HENRY
  RN: H.P. Lovecraft

PAIN, BARRY
  RN: Eric Odell

PALINURUS
  RN: Cyril Vernon Connolly

PAN
  RN: Leslie Beresford

PARABELLUM
  RN: Ferdinand Heinrich Grautoff

PARADICE, MARY
  RN: Dorothy Eden

PARIS, JOHN
  RN: Frank Ashton-Gwatkin

PARKES, WYNDHAM
  RN: John Baynen Harris

PARR, ROBERT
  RN: Erle Stanley Gardner

PARTRIDGE, ANTHONY
  RN: E. Phillips Oppenheim

PASSANTE, DOM
  RN: John Russell Fearn

PATRICK, KEATS
  RN: Walter Karig

PATRIOT, A.
  RN: L. Guy

PAYNE, GUTHRIE
  RN: F. Orlin Tremaine

PAYTON, GREEN
  RN: G. Payton Wertenbaker

PEARSON, MARTIN
  RN: Don Wollheim

PEASE, LT. JOHN
  RN: Roger Sherman Hoar

PECCAVI
  RN: Robert Graves

PEDDIWELL, J. ABNER
  RN: Harold R.W. Benjamin

PELKIE, JOE W(alter)
  RN: Raymond A. Palmer

PENDARVES, G.G.
  RN: Gladys Gordon Trenery

PENMARE, WILLIAM
  RN: Mrs. Mavis E. Nisot

PENTECOST, HUGH
  RN: Judson Philips

PEREGOY, CALVIN
  RN: Thomas Calvert McClary

PERKINS, ELI
  RN: Melville D. Landon

PERROT, GERVASE
  RN: Arthur Machen

PETERS, BILL
  RN: William P. McGivern

PETERS, ELLIS
  RN: Edith Pargeter

PHELAN, JEREMIAH
  RN: C. Daly King

PHELPS, FREDERICK
  RN: Johnston McCulley

PHILLIPS, FRANK
  RN: Phil Nowlan

PHILLIPS, ROG
  RN: Roger P. Graham

PHILLIPS, STEVE
  RN: Harry Whittington

PHILLIPS, WARD
  RN: H.P. Lovecraft

PHYLOS THE TIBETAN
  RN: F.S. Oliver

PIKE, ROBERT L.
  RN: Robert L. Fish

PILIBIN, AN
  RN: John Pollock

PINE, THEODORE
  RN: Emil Petaja

PLAIDY, JEAN
  RN: Eleanor Burford Hibbert

PLANET PRINCE, THE
  RN: J. Harvey Haggard

PORLOCK, MARTIN
  RN: Philip MacDonald

POWELL, SONNY
  RN: Alfred Bester

PRESTON, ARTHUR
  RN: Frederick Faust

PRIME, LORD, ESQ.
  RN: Walter D. Reynolds

PRUNING KNIFE
  RN: Henry F. Allen

PSEUDOMAN, AKKAD
  RN: Edwin F. Northrup

PURVIS, CLEMENT
  RN: Gardner F. Fox

PUTNAM, ISRA
  RN: Greya La Spina

PUTNAM, J. WESLEY
  RN: Henry Sinclair Drago

Q
  RN: Sir Arthur Quiller-Couch

QUARRY, NICK
  RN: Marvin H. Albert

QUEEN, ELLERY, JR.
  RN: James Clark Carlisle Holding, Jr.

QUIEN SABE
  RN: Harry Bates
  RN: Jackson Gregory
  (This PN was used independently by both Bates & Gregory.)

QUITMAN, WALLACE
  RN: Raymond A. Palmer

RACKHAM, JOHN
  RN: John T. Phillifent

RAGGED, HYDER
  RN: Henry C. Biron

RAINEY, WILLIAM
  RN: Wyatt Blassinghame

RALEIGH, RICHARD
  RN: H.P. Lovecraft

RALEY, ROWENA
  RN: Johnstone McCulley

RAMAL, WALTER
  RN: Walter de la Mare

RAME, DAVID
  RN: Arthur Durham Divine

RANGER, KEN
  RN: John Creasey

RANKINE, JOHN
  RN: Douglas Mason

RANSOME, STEPHEN
  RN: Frederick Clyde Davis

RAY, JEAN
  RN: Raymond De Kremer

RAYCRAFT, STAN
  RN: Richard S. Shaver

RAYMOND, E.V.
  RN: Raymond Z. Gallun

RAYMOND, HUGH
  RN: John Michel

RAYNER, RICHARD
  RN: David McIlwain

RECOUR, CHARLES
  RN: Henry Bott

REED, ALAN
  RN: Wolf Detlef Rohr

REED, DAVID V.
  RN: David Vern

REED, PETER
  RN: John D. MacDonald

REES, DILWYN
  RN: Glyn Edmund Daniel

REILLY, WILLIAM K.
  RN: John Creasey

REMENHAM, JOHN
  RN: J.A. Vlasto

RENAULT, MARY
  RN: Mary Challans

RERSLEY (ROWLEY), AMES DORRANCE
  RN: H.P. Lovecraft

REY, CAROL
  RN: Robert W. Lowndes

REYNOLDS, ADRIAN
  RN: Amelia Reynolds Long

REYNOLDS, L. MAJOR
  RN: Louise Leipiar

REYNOLDS, MACK
  RN: Dallas McCord Reynolds

REYNOLDS, MAXINE
  RN: Dallas McCord Reynolds

REYNOLDS, PETER
  RN: Amelia Reynolds Long

RHODAN, FORRY
  RN: Forrest J. Ackerman

RHODE, JOHN
  RN: Cecil John Charles Street

RICE, CRAIG
  RN: Georgiana Ann Randall

RICHARDS, CLAY
  RN: Kendall Foster Crossen

RICHARDS, HENRY
  RN: Richard Saxon

RICHARDSON, FLAVIA
  RN: Christine Campbell Thomson

RICHMOND, GRACE
  RN: John Marsh

RICHMOND, ROD
  RN: Donald Frank Glut

RIDDELL, JOHN
  RN: Corey Ford

RIESER, HENRY
  RN: John D. MacDonald

RIKER, ANTHONY
  RN: F. Anton Reeds

RILEY, TEX
  RN: John Creasey

RIOS, TERE
  RN: Maria Theresa Rios Versack

RIVERS, ELFREIDA
  RN: Marion Zimmer Bradley

RIVERSIDE, JOHN
  RN: Robert A. Heinlein

RIVERTON, STEIN
  RN: Sven Elvstad

ROBBINS, W. WAYNE
  RN: Ormond Gregory

ROBERTS, LIONEL
  RN: Robert Lionel Fanthorpe

ROBERTS, TERENCE
  RN: Ivan T. Sanderson

ROBERTS, WAYNE
  RN: Wayne D. Overholser

ROBINETT, LEE
  RN: Robert A. Bennett

ROCKINGHAM, MONTAGUE
  RN: Nelson Coral Nye

RODMAN, ERIC
  RN: Robert Silverberg

ROGER, NOELLE
  RN: Helene Pittard

ROGERS, MELVA
  RN: Roger P. Graham

ROGERS, MICK
  RN: Donald Frank Glut

ROHMER, ELIZABETH SAX
  RN: Rose Elizabeth Knox Ward

ROHMER, SAX
  RN: Arthur Salsfield Ward

ROME, ANTHONY
  RN: Marvin H. Albert

RONNS, E.S.
  RN: Edward S. Aarons

ROSE, FRANCIS
  RN: John Russell Fearn

ROSE, L.F.
  RN: John Russell Fearn

ROSE, LAURENCE
  RN: John Russell Fearn

ROSNEY, J.H. AINE
  RN: J.H.H. Boex

ROSS, AIRCRAFTSMAN
  RN: Thomas Edward Lawrence

ROSS, ALBERT
  RN: Linn B. Porter

ROSS, CLARISSA
  RN: Dan Ross

ROSS, DALLAS
  RN: Dallas McCord Reynolds

ROSS, JONATHAN
  RN: John Rossiter

ROSS, JOSEPH
  RN: Joseph Wrocz

ROSS, MARILYN
  RN: Dan Ross

ROSS, WARD
  RN: John Russell Fearn

ROUSSEAU, VICTOR
  RN: Victor Rousseau Emmanuel

RUPERT, CHESTER
  RN: Roger P. Graham

RUSSELL, ALBERT
  RN: Jerome Bixby

RUSSELL, ARTHUR
  RN: Arthur Russell Goode

RUSSELL, J.
  RN: Jerome Bixby

RUTLEDGE, MARYSE
  RN: Marice R. Hale

RYAN, AL
  RN: Durham Keith Garton

RYAN, TIM
  RN: Lester Dent

RYAN, WALTER
  RN: Walt Willis

S., R.
  RN: Robert Paltock

SADEUR, JAMES
  RN: Gabriel DeFoigny

SAEGAR, JOAN
  RN: John Russell Fearn

SAINT-AUBIN, HORACE de
  RN: Honoré de Balzac

ST. JOHN, PHILIP
  RN: Lester del Rey

ST. JOHN, RANDOLPH
  RN: Rheinhart Kleiner

ST. LUZ, BERTHE
  RN: Alice A. Robertson

ST. PAUL, STERNER
  RN: Capt. Sterner St. Paul Meek

ST. REYNARD, GEOFF
  RN: Robert W. Krepps

ST. VIVANT, M.
  RN: Jerome Bixby

SAKI
  RN: Hector Hugh Munro

SANBORN, B.X.
  RN: William S. Ballinger

SAND, WARREN B.
  RN: F. Orlin Tremaine

SANDERS, DAPHNE
  RN: Georgiana Ann Randall

SANDERS, WINSTON P.
  RN: Poul Anderson

SANDYS, OLIVER
  RN: Florence L. Barclay

SANTOS, ALFRED
  RN: F. Orlin Tremaine

SAPPER
  RN: Gerard T. Farlie
  RN: H.C. McNeile
  (Farlie used the Sapper PN after McNeile's death.)

SARBAN
  RN: John W. Wall

SAUNDERS, CALEB
  RN: Robert A. Heinlein

SAVA, GEORGE
  RN: Alexis Milkomanovich Milkomane

SAVAGE, RICHARD
  RN: Ivan Roe

SAXON, ALEX
  RN: William Pronzini

SCOTLAND, JAY
  RN: John Jakes

SCOTT, ANTHONY
  RN: Davis Dresser

SCOTT, BRADFORD
  RN: A. Leslie

SCOTT, JEREMY
  RN: Kay Dick

SEABORN, CAPT. ADAM
  RN: John Cleaves Symmes

SEABRIGHT, IDRIS
  RN: Margaret St. Clair

SEABROOK, JOHN
  RN: L. Ron Hubbard

SEAFORTH
  RN: George Cecil Foster

SEAFORTH, A. NELSON
  RN: George S. Clarke

SEAMARK
  RN: Austin Small

SEBASTIAN, LEE
  RN: Robert Silverberg

SELLINGS, ARTHUR
  RN: Arthur Ley

SEUSS, DR.
  RN: Theodore Seuss Geisel

SEVERN, DAVID
  RN: David Storr Unwin

SEWELL, ARTHUR
  RN: John Harvey Whitson

SEYMOUR, ALLEN
  RN: Sydney Fowler Wright

SHADOW, MARK
  RN: Robert W. Sneddon

SHARON, ROSE
  RN: Josephine Judith Grossman

SHARP, LUKE
  RN: Robert Barr

SHARPE, D. RICHARD
  RN: Richard S. Shaver

SHAW, BRIAN
  RN: E.C. Tubb

SHAW, BRYAN
  RN: John Russell Fearn

SHAW, ROBERT SANDERS
  RN: Sam Moskowitz

SHAW, T.E.
  RN: Thomas Edward Lawrence

SHEAN, N.R.
  RN: M.P. Shiel

SHEARING, JOSEPH
  RN: Gabrielle Campbell

SHELDON, RACOONA
  RN: Alice Sheldon

SHELDON, ROY
  RN: E.C. Tubb

SHELLEY, PETER
  RN: Davis Dresser

SHELTON, MILES
  RN: Don Wilcox

SHEPHERD, JOHN
  RN: Willis Todhunter Ballard

SHERIDAN, THOMAS
  RN: Walter L. Gillings

SHERRY, OLIVER
  RN: George E. Lobo

SHERWOOD, NELSON
  RN: Kenneth Bulmer

SHORT, LUKE
  RN: Frederick Dilley Glidden

SHOTWELL, RAY P.
  RN: Ray Cummings

SHUTE, NEVIL
  RN: Nevil Shute Norway

SIDEN, CAPTAIN
  RN: Denis Vairasse

SIDNEY, EDWARD WILLIAM
  RN: Nathaniel Beverley Tucker

SILURIENSIS, LEOLINUS
  RN: Arthur Machen

SILVER, NICHOLAS
  RN: Frederick Faust

SIMS, LT. A.K.
  RN: John Harvey Whitson

SINBAD
  RN: Aylward E. Dingle

SINCLAIR, B.M.
  RN: Bertha Muzzy Bower

SINCLAIR, GRANT
  RN: Henry Sinclair Drago

SIRIUS
  RN: Edward Martyn

SIWAARMILL, H.P.
  RN: William Sharp

SLATE, JOHN
  RN: John Russell Fearn

SMITH, CARMICHAEL
  RN: Paul Linebarger

SMITH, CORDWAINER
  RN: Paul Linebarger

SMITH, FORD
  RN: Oscar J. Friend

SMITH, WOODROW WILSON
  RN: Henry Kuttner

SNOOKS, EPAMINONDAS T.
  RN: C.P. Mason

SOFTLY, EDWARD
  RN: H.P. Lovecraft

SOMERS, BART
  RN: Gardner F. Fox

SOMMERVILLE, FRANKFORT
  RN: A.M. Sommerville Story

SOUTH, CLARK
  RN: Dwight Vreeland Swain

SPAIN, JOHN
  RN: Cleve Franklin Adams

SPARLING, NED
  RN: Luis Philip Senarens

SPAULDING, LEONARD
  RN: Ray Bradbury

SPEKTOR, DR.
  RN: Donald Frank Glut

SPENCER, JOHN
  RN: Roy Vickers

SPENCER, PARKE
  RN: Sewell Peaseley Wright

SPIE, OLIVER
  RN: Joseph Slotkin

SPRAGUE, CARTER
  RN: Sam Merwin, Jr.

SQUARE, A.
  RN: Edwin A. Abbot

STACY, O'CONNER
  RN: William Stacy Uran Rollins

STAINES, TREVOR
  RN: John Brunner

STAIRS, GORDON
  RN: Mary Austin

STANLEY, BENNETT
  RN: Stanley Bennett Hough

STANLEY, MARGE
  RN: Stanley G. Weinbaum

STANTON, EDWARD
  RN: Edward S. Huntington

STANTON, JOHN
  RN: George C. Wallis

STARK, HENDERSON
  RN: Kris Neville

STARK, RICHARD
  RN: Donald E. Westlake

STARR, JOHN
  RN: Roger D. Aycock

STATON, VANCE
  RN: Michael Avallone

STATTEN, VARGO
  RN: John Russell Fearn

STAUNTON, SCHUYLER
  RN: L. Frank Baum

STEEL, ROBERT
  RN: John Harvey Whitson

STEELE, ADDISON
  RN: John Harvey Addison

STEELE, DALE
  RN: Donald Frank Glut

STEELE, MORRIS J.
  RN: Berkley Livingston

STEIGER, BRAD
  RN: Eugene E. Olson

STEPHENS, FRANCIS
  RN: Gertrude Bennett

STEPHENS, R.L.
  RN: Edward D. Hoch

STERN, PAUL FREDERICK
  RN: Paul Ernst

STEVENS, DAN J.
  RN: Wayne D. Overholser

STEVENS, MAURICE
  RN: John Harvey Whitson

STEWART, JAY
  RN: Stewart Palmer

STEWART, WILL
  RN: Jack Williamson

STODDARD, CHARLES
  RN: Henry Kuttner

STOKES, SIMPSON
  RN: Frank D. Fawcett

STONE, LESLEY F.
  RN: Mrs. William Silberberg

STORM, HARRISON
  RN: Bruno Fischer

STORM, RUSSELL
  RN: Robert Moore Williams

STRINGER, DAVID
  RN: Keith Roberts

STRONG, HARRINGTON
  RN: Johnston McCulley

STRONG, SPENSER
  RN: Forrest J. Ackerman

STUART, CLAY
  RN: Harry Whittington

STUART, DON A.
  RN: John W. Campbell, Jr.

STUART, IAN
  RN: Alistair Stuart MacLean

STUART, SIDNEY
  RN: Michael Avallone

STUDENT OF OCCULTISM, A
  RN: Franz Hartmann

SUTTER, PHILIP
  RN: Corwin Stickney

SWANSON, LOGAN
  RN: Richard Matheson

SWAYNE, MARTIN
  RN: Maurice Nicoll

SWEVEN, GODFREY
  RN: John Macmillan Brown

SWIFT, ANTHONY
  RN: Joseph Jefferson Farjeon

SWIFT, AUGUSTUS T.
  RN: H.P. Lovecraft

TAINE, JOHN
  RN: Eric Temple Bell

TANGENT, PATRICK Q.
  RN: George H. Phelps

TARNACRE, ROBERT
  RN: Robert Cartmell

TATE, ELLALICE
  RN: Eleanor Burford Hibbert

TAVEREL, JOHN
  RN: Robert E. Howard

TAYLOR, BRUCE
  RN: Leslie C.B. Lin

TEMPLE, JAMES
  RN: Eric Temple Bell

TEMPLE-ELLIS, N.A.
  RN: Neville Aldridge Holdaway

TENN, WILLIAM
  RN: Philip Klass

TERRIDGE, ERNEST
  RN: Ernst H. Richter

TERTZ, ABRAM
  RN: Andrei Donatevich Sinihvskii

TEY, JOSEPHINE
  RN: Elizabeth MacKintosh

THAMES, C.H.
  RN: Milton Lesser

136

THANET, OCTAVE
  RN: Alice French

THAYER, TIFFANY
  RN: Tiffany Ellsworth Thayer

THAYER, URANN
  RN: William Stacy Uran Rollins

THEOBALD, LEWIS, JR.
  RN: H.P. Lovecraft

THIUSEN, ISMAR
  RN: John MacNie

THOMAS, DAN
  RN: Leonard M. Sanders

THOMAS, DORIS
  RN: Doris Vancel

THOMAS, K.
  RN: John Russell Fearn

THOMAS, MARTIN
  RN: Thomas Hector Martin

THOMPSON, CHINA
  RN: Mary Christina Lewis

THORNE, BRADLEY D.
  RN: Donald Frank Glut

THORNE, GUY
  RN: Cyril A. Ranger Gull

THORNTON, HALL
  RN: Robert Silverberg

THORP, DOBBIN
  RN: Thomas Disch

THORPE, TREBOR
  RN: Robert Lionel Fanthorpe

THORSTEIN, ERIC
  RN: Josephine Judith Grossman

TILLRAY, LES
  RN: Erle Stanley Gardner

TILTON, ALICE
  RN: Phoebe Atwood Taylor

TIPTREE, JAMES, JR.
  RN: Alice Sheldon

TITAN, EARL
  RN: John Russell Fearn

TOBIAS, KATHERINE
  RN: Theodore Mark Gottfried

TOLZ, NICK
  RN: Joseph Slotkin

TOM, HUNG LONG
  RN: Roswell Williams

TORGOSI, VESPERTINA
  RN: Forrest J. Ackerman

TORLEY, LUKE
  RN: James Blish

TORRO, PEL
  RN: Robert Lionel Fanthorpe

TOWNE, STUART
  RN: Clayton Rawson

TRAPROCK, WALTER E.
  RN: George S. Chappell

TRAVEN, B.
  RN: Traven Torsvan

TRAVER, ROBERT
  RN: John Donaldson Voelke

TRENT, CLYVE
  RN: Victor Rousseau Emmanuel

TREVENA, JOHN
  RN: Ernest Henham

TROUT, KILGORE
  RN: Philip José Farmer

TURBOJEW, ALEXAI
  RN: Karl Herbert Scheer

TWAIN, MARK
  RN: Samuel L. Clemens

TYLER, THEODORE
  RN: Edward William Ziegler

TYSON, ARNOLD
  RN: Harold Hersey

UNDERWOOD, MICHAEL
  RN: John Michael Evelyn

URIEL, HENRY
  RN: Frederick Faust

USHER, MARGO SEESSE
  RN: Georgess McHargue

VAETH, MARTIN
  RN: Frederick Arnold Kummer

VALDING, VICTOR
  RN: Allen Ingvald Benson

VALENTINE, JO
  RN: Charlotte Armstrong

VANCE, GEOFFREY
  RN: Hugh B. Cave

VANCE, JACK
  RN: John Holbrook Vance
  (See also Gerald Vance & Henry Kuttner, Section I.)

Van DINE, S.S.
  RN: Willard (Huntington) Wright

Van DYNE, EDITH
  RN: L. Frank Baum

Van LHIN, ERIK
  RN: Lester del Rey

Van LORNE, WARNER
  RN: F. Orlin Tremaine

VANSHUCK, GREGO
  RN: Hugo Gernsback

VARA, MADELEINE
  RN: Laura Riding

VARDON, RICHARD
  RN: David Wright O'Brien

VEDDER, JOHN K.
  RN: Frank Gruber

VELLIN, EDWARD J.
  RN: Henry Kuttner

VENNING, MICHAEL
  RN: Georgiana Ann Randall

VERCORS
  RN: Cyril Vernon Connolly

VERCORS, JEAN
  RN: Jean Bruller

VERETT, H.E.
  RN: E. Everett Evans

VERNON, VAIL
  RN: Harold Hersey

VILLETTE, ALLIS
  RN: Forrest J. Ackerman

VINCENT, HARL
  RN: Harl Vincent Schoepflin

VonDREY, HOWARD
  RN: Howard E. Wandrei

Von HELDERS, MAJOR
  RN: Robert Knauss

Von HIMMEL, ERNST
  RN: Carlyle Petersilea

VonRACHEN, KURT
  RN: L. Ron Hubbard

VOYANT, CLAIRE
  RN: Forrest J. Ackerman

W., N.
  RN: C.S. Lewis

WALDO, E. HUNTER
  RN: Theodore Sturgeon

WALES, HUBERT
  RN: William Piggott

WALLACE, IAN
  RN: John Pritchard

WALSER, SAM
  RN: Robert E. Howard

WALSEY, CHARNOCK
  RN: Les Heald

WALTERS, SELDON
  RN: Walt Sheldon

WARD, HENRY
  RN: Henri Viard

WARLAND, ALLEN
  RN: Don Wollheim

WARWICK, GEORGE
  RN: George Warwick Deeping

WATER, SILAS
  RN: Noel Loomis

WATERHOUSE, ARTHUR
  RN: John Russell Fearn

WATSON, RICHARD F.
  RN: Robert Silverberg

WAYNE, ANDERSON
  RN: Davis Dresser

WAYNE, JOSEPH
  RN: Wayne D. Overholser

WAYNE, RAYMOND
  RN: Harold R.W. Benjamin

WEAVER, WARD
  RN: Francis Van Wyck Mason

WEBSTER, ROBERT N.
  RN: Ray Palmer

WEINER, WILLIAM M.
  RN: Sam Moskowitz

WEIR, MORDRED
  RN: Amelia Reynolds Long

WELLES, BRAXTON
  RN: Don Wollheim

WELLES, HUBERT GEORGE
  RN: Forrest J. Ackerman

WELLS, HONDO
  RN: Harry Whittington

WELLS, J. WENTWORTH
  RN: L. Sprague De Camp

WELLS, JOHN JAY
  RN: Juanita Coulson

WENTWORTH, PATRICIA
  RN: Dora A. Dillon

WENTWORTH, ROBERT
  RN: Edmund Hamilton

WEST, MICHAEL
  RN: August Derleth

WESTLAND, LYNN
  RN: Archie L. Joscelyn

WESTMACOTT, MARY
  RN: Agatha Christie

WESTON, ALLEN
  RN: Alice Mary Norton

WHILK, NAT
  RN: C.S. Lewis

WHITE, HARRY
  RN: Harry Whittington

WHITE, PARKER
  RN: William Anthony Parker White

WHITLEY, GEORGE
  RN: A. Bertram Chandler

WHITNEY, HALLAM
  RN: Harry Whittington

WHITNEY, SPENCER
  RN: Arthur J. Burkes

WILEY, DIRK
  RN: Cyril M. Kornbluth

WILEY, JOHN
  RN: Roger P. Graham

WILLEY, ROBERT
  RN: Willy Ley

WILLIAMS, RUSSELL
  RN: John Harvey Whitson

WILLIAMS, SPEEDY
  RN: L.H. Smith

WILLIAMS, TENNESSEE
  RN: Thomas Lanier Williams

WILLIE, ALBERT FREDERICK
  RN: H.P. Lovecraft

WILLIS, CHARLES
  RN: Arthur C. Clarke

WILLY THE WISP
  RN: Don Wollheim

WILSON, GABRIEL
  RN: Ray Cummings

WILSON, JOHN BURGESS
  RN: John Anthony Burgess Wilson

WINIKI, EPHRAIM
  RN: John Russell Fearn

WINTER, H.G.
  RN: Harry Bates

WINTER, R.R.
  RN: Russ Winterbotham

WINTERS, RAE
  RN: Raymond A. Palmer

WINTERTON, GALE
  RN: William T. Adams

WINWAR, FRANCES
  RN: Frances V. Grebanier

WOE, WILLIS W.
  RN: Wilson Shepard

WOLLONOVER, FRED
  RN: Sam Moskowitz

WONDER, WILLIAM
  RN: Thomas Kirwan

WOODCOTT, KEITH
  RN: John Brunner

WOODRUFF, CLYDE
  RN: David Vern

WOODWARD, LILLIAN
  RN: John Marsh

WOOLFOLK, JOSIAH PITTS
  RN: Jack Woodford

WORTH, AMY
  RN: David H. Keller

WORTH, NIGEL
  RN: Noel Wright

WRIGHT, WEAVER
  RN: Forrest J. Ackerman

WYCLIFFE, JOHN
  RN: Henry James O'Brien Bedford-Jones

WYLIE, DIRK
  RN: Harry Dockweiler

WYLWYNNE, KYTHE
  RN: M.E.F. Hyland

WYNDHAM, JOHN
  RN: John Baynen Harris

"X"
  RN: Don Wollheim

X, EX-PRIVATE
  RN: Alfred McClelland Burrage

X, GENERAL
  RN: Roger Sherman Hoar

X, MISTER
  RN: Edward D. Hoch

X.X.
  RN: Cecil John Charles Street

YATES, DORNFORD
  RN: Cecil W. Mercer

YORK, JEREMY
  RN: John Creasey

YORKE, SIMON
  RN: Robert A. Heinlein

YOUNG, COLLIER
  RN: Robert Bloch

YOUNG, RAYMOND A.
  RN: Vernon Jones

Z
  RN: Robert Graves

ZACKERLEY
  RN: John Zacherle

ZAROVITCH, VERA
  RN: Mary E. Lane

ZETFORD, TULLY
  RN: Kenneth H. Bulmer

ZOILUS
  RN: H.P. Lovecraft

ZWEIG, ALAN
  RN: Frederik Pohl

SECTION III

COLLABORATIVE PEN NAMES (CPN)

These are defined as the private writing names of
two or more individual authors writing in partnership.

ASHDOWN, CLIFFORD
  Richard Austin Freeman & John James Pitcairn

BARBETTE, JAY
  Bart Spicer & Betty Spicer

BAXTER, GREGORY
  Eric De Banzie & John Ressich

BEEDING, FRANCIS
  John Leslie Palmer & Hilary Aidan St. George Saunders

BINDER, EANDO
  Earl Binder & Otto Binder

BIRD, BRANDON
  George Evans & Kay Evans

COLERIDGE, JOHN
  Earl Binder & Otto Binder

COLES, MANNING
  Adelaide F.O. Manning & Cyril Henry Coles

COOKE, ARTHUR
  (This was a 5-way CPN for E. Balter, Cyril Kornbluth,
    Robert W. Lowndes, John Michel & Don Wollheim.)

COX, KATHLEEN BUDDINGTON
  Amelia Reynolds Long & Edna McHugh

DAMONTI, HENRI
  Mr. & Mrs. Smolarski
  (Damonti was a CPN for a husband-and-wife team, writing in
    French. Their translator was Damon Knight, but Knight
    did not use the Damonti CPN in any of his own writings.)

DEBRETT, HAL
  Davis Dresser & Kathleen Rollins

145

DEER, M.J.
  M. Jane Deer & George H. Smith

DEMIJOHN, THOM
  Thomas Disch & John Sladek

DOLBOKOV
  Boris Dolgov & Wayne Woodard

EATON, GEORGE
  Monte Montayne & Chuck Verral

EDWARDS, NORMAN
  Terry Carr & Ted White

ELDERSHAW, M. BARNARD
  Marjorie Faith Barnard & Flora Sydney Patricia Eldershaw

ELLANBOY, BOYD
  Lyle U. Boyd & William C. Boyd

FLEMING, OLIVER
  Philip MacDonald & Ronald MacDonald

FORSTO, MIRTA
  Forrest J. Ackerman & Myrtle R. Douglas

GAITE, FRANCIS
  Cyril Henry Coles & Adelaide F.O. Manning

GILMORE, ANTHONY
  Harry Bates & Desmond Hall
  (In the 1940's, the Gilmore CPN was used as a PN by Bates
    alone.)

GOTTESMAN, S.D.
  Cyril M. Kornbluth, Robert Lowndes & Frederik Pohl
  (The Gottesman CPN was used as a private PN by Kornbluth,
    as a CPN between Kornbluth & Pohl, and as a 3-way CPN
    by Kornbluth, Lowndes & Pohl.)

HAMMOND, KEITH
  Henry Kuttner & C.L. Moore

HASTINGS, HUDSON
  Henry Kuttner & C.L. Moore

HERON, E. & H.
  Kate Prichard & Hesketh Prichard

HOLMES, GORDON
  M.P. Shiel & Louis Tracy
  (This was a CPN for detective stories. Tracy also used it
    for some solo efforts. See M.P. Shiel in Section I.)

JOHNS, KENNETH
  Kenneth Bulmer & John Newman

JUDD, CYRIL
  Cyril Kornbluth & Josephine Judith Grossman

KEITH, DONALD
  Donald Monroe & Keith Monroe

LAVERTY, DONALD
  James Blish & Damon Knight

LaVOND, PAUL DENNIS
  Cyril M. Kornbluth, Robert W. Lowndes, Frederik Pohl &
  Harry Dockweiler
  (This was used in one solo effort by Lowndes, and various
    complex collaborations among Kornbluth, Lowndes & Dock-
    weiler, now almost impossible to sort out.)

LESLIE, WILLIAM
  Archer Hood & Violet Perkins

LIDDELL, C.H.
  Henry Kuttner & C.L. Moore

LINCOLN, FAITH
  Ed Reed, Frank Lunney & Leo Doroschenko

LORAN, MARTIN
  John Baxter & Ron Smith

McCANN, EDSON
  Lester del Rey & Frederik Pohl

McCARTER, JODY
  Jodi De Melikoff & Ver Mille McCarter

McDERMOTT, DENNIS
  P. Schuyler Miller, Walter Dennis & Paul McDermott
  (This CPN was also used separately by Miller.)

McDONALD, RAYMOND
  Raymond A. Leger & Edward R. McDonald

MacDOUGAL, JOHN
  Robert W. Lowndes & James Blish

MASON, GREGORY
  Doris Meek & Adrienne Jones

MASTERSON, WHIT
  Robert Miller & Robert Wade

MILLER, WADE
  Robert Miller & Robert Wade

NAVARCHUS
    Patrick Vaux & Lionel Yexley

O'BRIEN, DEAN D.
    Earl Binder & Otto Binder

O'DONNELL, LAURENCE
    Henry Kuttner & C.L. Moore

PADGETT, LEWIS
    Henry Kuttner & C.L. Moore

PARK, JORDAN
    Cyril M. Kornbluth & Frederik Pohl

PATRICK, Q.
    Richard Webb & Hugh C. Wheeler

PHILLIPS, MARK
    Randall Garrett & Larry M. Harris

PROSPERO & CALIBAN
    C.H.C. Pirie-Gordon & Frederick W. Rolfe

QUEEN, ELLERY
    Frederick Dannay & Manfred Lee
    (See also Paul W. Fairman in Section I.)

QUENTIN, PATRICK
    Richard Webb & Hugh C. Wheeler

RANDALL, ROBERT
    Randall Garrett & Robert Silverberg

REED, ELIOT
    Eric Ambler & Charles Rodda

RICH, BARBARA
    Robert Graves & Laura Riding

RICHARD-BESSIERE, F.
    Richard Bessiere & François Richard

ROSS, BARNABY
    Frederick Dannay & Manfred Lee

SABEN, GREGORY
    Gertrude Saben & Frederick Burkitt

STAGG, JONATHAN
    Richard Webb & Hugh C. Wheeler

STANDISH, BURT
    William Gilbert Patten & John Harvey Whitson

STRANG, HERBERT
    George Ely & C.J. L'Estrange

STRATTON, THOMAS
  Robert Coulson & Gene De Wease

TWO WAGS
  John Kendrick Bangs & Frank D. Sherman

WERPER, BARTON
  Peter T. Scott & Peggy O. Scott

WINTER, H.G.
  Harry Bates & Desmond Hall

WOODS, LAWRENCE
  John Michel, Robert W. Lowndes & Don Wollheim
  (This was also used as a separate PN by Wollheim.)

SECTION IV

HOUSE NAMES (HN)

HOUSE NAMES are defined as those writing names
created by a publishing house or firm, and used
exclusively by writers creating material for that
house or firm.

This section lists each HN alphabetically along
with the publishing house, followed by the series
character and magazine title, where this is appli-
cable, and the real name of each writer who used
the HN. Neither Ziff-Davis, which did not use
single-character magazines, nor the British HN's,
have this breakdown.

NOTE: BRE signifies British Edition.

AGHILL, GORDON (Ziff-Davis)
   Randall Garrett
   Robert Silverberg

ARCHER, LEE (Ziff-Davis)
   Harlan Ellison

ARNETT, ROBERT (Ziff-Davis)
   Roger P. Graham
   Robert Silverberg

BAHL, FRANKLIN (Ziff-Davis)
   Roger P. Graham

BENTON, JOHN (Better): Jerry Wade Series / Detective Novels
   Norman Dannenberg

BLADE, ALEXANDER (Ziff-Davis; Palmer; Greenleaf)
   Howard Browne
   Millen Cooke
   Randall Garrett
   Chester S. Geier

BLADE, ALEXANDER (cont'd)
  Roger P. Graham
  Edmund Hamilton
  Heinrich Hauser
  Berkley Livingston
  Herb Livingston
  William P. McGivern
  David Wright O'Brien
  Louis H. Sampliner
  Richard S. Shaver
  Robert Silverberg
  David Vern
  Don Wilcox
  Leroy Yerxa

BLAKE, SEXTON (BRE)
    Sexton Blake was the hero of a British detective series
created by Harry Blyth under the name of Hal Meredith on
Dec. 20, 1893. The Sexton Blake character seems to have
resembled America's Nick Carter and, like him, survives
into the present day through series novels in the SEXTON
BLAKE LIBRARY, after publication in a variety of magazines
over the years. Since there were some 200 authors con-
tributing to the approximately 4,000 separate titles in
this series, HN identification is as yet possible only in
a few widely scattered cases. The confusion is not allevi-
ated by the publisher's habit of switching back and forth
between HN's and RN's.
    Perhaps this entry can form the basis for a more complete
notation of author identities as more information becomes
available from the publisher.
    The following authors wrote stories and books about
Sexton Blake:

Harry Blyth, writing as Hal Meredith: 1852-1898
Edwy Searles Brooks: 1889-1965
Jack Lewis: fl. c. 1933

    The following authors wrote SEXTON BLAKE LIBRARY series
novels around the years 1959-1962:

W. Howard Baker
Jim Cawthorn, under HN of Desmond Reid
Philip Chambers, under HN of Desmond Reid
Philip Chambliss, under HN of Desmond Reid
John Newton Chance, under HN of Desmond Reid
Rex Hardinge
Christopher Lowder
George Mann, under HN of Arthur MacLean
Michael Moorcock, under HN of Desmond Reid
E.C. Tubb, under HN of Arthur MacLean

BRENGLE, WILLIAM (Ziff-Davis)
  Howard Browne

BROOKER, WALLACE (Street & Smith): The Skipper Series / The
    Skipper Magazine; Doc Savage Magazine
  William Bogart
  Norman Dannenberg
  Laurence Donovan

BURKE, RALPH (Ziff-Davis; Greenleaf)
  Randall Garrett
  Robert Silverberg

BURNS, TEX (Better; Doubleday)
  (The Tex Burns HN was created for the commissioned Hopalong
    Cassidy novels. The first 2 novels appeared in magazines,
    and all 4 novels were published in hardback under this
    HN.)
  Louis L'Amour

CARLETON, H.B. (Ziff-Davis)
  Howard Browne

CARTER, NICK (Street & Smith)
    If sheer volume and duration mean anything, then surely a
  prime contender for the title of King of House Names must
  be Detective Nick Carter, whose publishing history as of
  this writing (1980) extends back more than 90 years. This
  also makes the Carter HN one of the most confusing to trace
  throughout the different publishing media.
    Although his first appearance is still uncertain, Nick
  Carter was appearing in the story papers, specifically the
  New York Weekly, c. 1886.
    In 1891, the NICK CARTER DETECTIVE LIBRARY, a dime novel
  series, began, with the following writers writing *books*
  under this HN:

  William Wallace Cook: 1867-1933
  John Russell Coryell: 1848-1924
  (Although Coryell is credited with creating the Nick Carter
    character, it is uncertain whether this refers to the dime
    novel byline, or includes the earlier story paper
    character.)
  Frederick W. Davis: 1853-1933
  Frederick Van Rensselaer Dey: 1861-1922
  W. Bert Foster: 1869-1929
  Thomas W. Hanshew: 1857-1914
  Thomas C. Harbaugh: 1849-1924
  George C. Jenks: 1850-1929

CARTER, NICK (cont'd)
  Johnston McCulley: 1883-1958
  Eugene T. Sawyer: 1846-1924
  John W. Whitson: 1854-1936

  In 1933, Nick Carter began a new life as a Pulp Single
Character in the *Nick Carter Detective* pulp, which bowed
out in 1936, after a 40-issue run. The *novels* in each
issue were written by:

  John Chambliss
  T. Henderson
  Thomas Calvert McClary
  Richard Wormser

  In 1934, *Nick Carter Detective* introduced a series of
novelettes into the magazine, in addition to the lead novels.
These *novelettes* were written by:

  John Chambliss
  Philip Clark

  Although they did not collaborate, both Chambliss and
Clark used the secondary HN of Harrison Keith for these
novelettes. Why Street & Smith should have introduced a
secondary HN at this time is problematical--possibly to
avoid confusion?
  In 1944, *The Shadow* introduced another series of Nick
Carter novels into its own pulp. These novels were written
by:

  Bruce Elliot

  In 1975, Award Books attempted to revive the Nick Carter
character, refurbished as a James Bond-type of secret agent,
with the code name "Killmaster." As of 1979 approximately
40 novels had appeared in this new series, but the writers
are uncertain. However, the debut novel in this series
was written by:

  Michael Avallone

CHANCE, GEORGE (Thrilling): Green Ghost Series / Green
    Magazine; The Ghost
  G.T. Fleming-Roberts

CHANDLER, LAWRENCE (Ziff-Davis)
  Howard Browne

CHASE, ADAM (Ziff-Davis)
  Paul W. Fairman
  Milton Lesser

CLAY, BERTHA (Street & Smith): dime novels
  John Russell Coryell

COBURN, L.J. (BRE / Badger)
  John Harvey
  Laurence James

COLE, JACKSON (Thrilling): Jim Hatfield Series / Texas Rangers
  Tom Curry
  A. Leslie

COSTELLO, P.F. (Ziff-Davis)
  Chester S. Geier
  Roger P. Graham

CRAIG, RANDOLPH (Popular): Octopus Series & Scorpion Series /
    Octopus Magazine; Scorpion Magazine
  Norvell Page

CURRIO, TYMAN (Street & Smith): dime novels
  John Russell Coryell

DANCER, J.B. (BRE / Badger)
  John Harvey
  Angus Wells

DAVIES, FREDERICK (Ace): Man from U.N.C.L.E. Series / Man
    from U.N.C.L.E.
  Ronald D. Ellik

DRAYTON, LILLIAN R. (Street & Smith): dime novels
  John Russell Coryell

DRUMMOND, JOHN PETER (Fiction House): Ki-Gor Series / Jungle
    Stories
  Stanley Mullen

EATON, GEORGE (Street & Smith): Bill Barnes Series / Air
    Adventures
  Monte Montayne
  Chuck Verral

EDWARDS, JULIA (Street & Smith): dime novels
  John Russell Coryell

ELLIS, CRAIG (Ziff-Davis)
  Lee Rogow
  David Vern

EVANS, JOHN (Ziff-Davis)
  Howard Browne

FLEMING, GERALDINE (Street & Smith): dime novels
  John Russell Coryell

FRANCIS, LEE (Ziff-Davis)
  Howard Browne

FRAZIER, ARTHUR (BRE / Badger)
  Kenneth Bulmer
  Laurence James

GADE, HENRY (Ziff-Davis)
  Raymond A. Palmer

GARSON, CLEE (Ziff-Davis)
  Paul W. Fairman
  David Wright O'Brien

GARRETT, CHARLES C. (BRE / Badger)
  Laurence James
  Angus Wells

GARTH, WILL (Thrilling)
  Otto Binder
  Edmund Hamilton
  Henry Kuttner
  Mort Weisinger

GOODRICH, CLIFFORD (Street & Smith): The Whisperer Series /
    The Whisperer Magazine
  Laurence Donovan
  Alan Hathway

GRANT, MARGARET (Street & Smith): dime novels
  John Russell Coryell

GRANT, MAXWELL (Street & Smith): The Shadow Series / The
    Shadow Magazine
  Lester Dent
  Bruce Elliot
  Walter D. Gibson
  Dennis Lynds (Lynds used this HN *only* on Belmont paperback
    originals, 1963-1967.)
  Theodore Tinsley

GREER, RICHARD (Ziff-Davis)
  Randall Garrett
  Robert Silverberg

GRIDBAN, VOLSTED (BRE)
  John Russell Fearn
  E.C. Tubb

GRIDLEY, AUSTIN (BRE)
  Laurence Donovan

GUNN, TOM
  Frank Gruber

HAWKS, CHESTER (Ace): Capt. Hazard Series / Capt. Hazard
    Magazine
  Paul Chadwick

HORN, PETER (Ziff-Davis)
  Henry Kuttner
  David Vern

HOUSE, BRANT (Wyn): Secret Agent X Series / Secret Agent X
    Magazine
  Paul Chadwick
  G.T. Fleming-Roberts
  R.T.M. Scott
  Arthur Leo Zagat

HOWARD, BARBARA (Street & Smith): dime novels
  John Russell Coryell

IRWIN, G.H. (Ziff-Davis)
  Raymond A. Palmer
  Richard S. Shaver

JAMES, WILLIAM M. (BRE / Badger)
  Terry Harknett
  Laurence James

JARVIS, E.K. (Ziff-Davis)
  Paul W. Fairman
  Robert Silverberg
  Robert Moore Williams

JONES, G. WAYMAN (Thrilling)
  Edwin Burkhilder
  D.L. Champion

JONES, G. WAYMAN (cont'd)
  Norman Dannenberg
  Jack D'Arcy
  Anatole France Feldman
  G.T. Fleming-Roberts
  Stewart Sterling

JORGENSON, IVAR (Ziff-Davis; Greenleaf)
  Paul W. Fairman
  Randall Garrett
  Robert Silverberg

KASTEL, WAREN (Ziff-Davis; Greenleaf)
  Chester S. Geier
  Robert Silverberg

KELLEY, BRIAN JAMES (Dell)
  F.H. Martin

KENT, KELVIN (Thrilling)
  Arthur K. Barnes
  Henry Kuttner

KIRK, RICHARD (BRE / Badger)
  Rob Holdstock
  Angus Wells

LANGHOLM, NEIL (BRE / Badger)
  Laurence James

LEE, CHARLES (Palmer)
  Roger P. Graham

LOHMAN, PAUL (Ziff-Davis)
  Richard S. Shaver

McLAGLEN, JOHN J. (BRE / Badger)
  John Harvey
  Laurence James

MANN, MILTON (Palmer)
  Roger P. Graham

MILMAN, HARRY DUBOIS (Street & Smith): dime novels
  John Russell Coryell

MITCHELL, CLYDE (Ziff-Davis)
  Randall Garrett
  Robert Silverberg

MORGAN, LT. SCOTT (Better): Lone Eagle Series / Lone Eagle
    Magazine; American Eagle Magazine
  Robert Sidney Bowen
  Norman Dannenberg
  F.E. Reichnitzer

MULLER, JOHN E. (BRE)
  Robert Lionel Fanthorpe

PATTON, FRANK (Ziff-Davis; Palmer)
  Raymond A. Palmer
  Richard S. Shaver

PIKE, CHARLES R. (BRE / Badger)
  Terry Harknett
  Angus Wells

POLLARD, JOHN X. (Ziff-Davis)
  Howard Browne

QUARTERMAN, MILTON (Street & Smith): dime novels
  John Russell Coryell

ROBERTS, KENNETH (Street & Smith): Doc Savage Series / Doc
    Savage Magazine
  Lester Dent
  (This HN has no connection with the writer of historical
    romances. When Doc Savage was in the planning stage, the
    publishers picked an HN out of the blue, "Kenneth Roberts."
    This was used as an HN for the first Doc Savage story
    only, in the March 1933 1/1 issue. When it was pointed
    out that Kenneth Roberts was already the well-established
    name of an accredited author, the publishers quickly
    altered their HN to Kenneth Robeson [see following entry].)

ROBESON, KENNETH (Street & Smith): Doc Savage Series; The
    Avenger Series / Doc Savage Magazine; The Avenger Magazine
  William Bogart
  Norman Dannenberg
  Harold A. Davis
  Lester Dent
  Laurence Donovan
  Paul Ernst
  Ron Goulart
  Alan Hathway
  Walter Ryerson Johnson
  Emil Tepperman

RUSSELL, LUCY MAY (Street & Smith): dime novels
  John Russell Coryell

SANDS, DAVE
  Bryce Walton
  (The Sands HN was also used outside the pulp field by
  Walton and others.)

SATTERFIELD, CHARLES (Galaxy)
  Lester del Rey
  Frederik Pohl

SAWTELLE, WILLIAM CARTER (Ziff-Davis)
  Roger P. Graham

SAXON, PETER (BRE)
  Thomas Hector Martin

SCANLON, C.K.M. (Thrilling): Dan Fowler Series / G-Men
    Detective Magazine
  George Fielding Eliot
  Frank Gruber

SPENCER, LEONARD G. (Ziff-Davis)
  Randall Garrett
  Robert Silverberg

STEBER, ALFRED R. (Ziff-Davis; Palmer)
  Roger P. Graham
  Raymond A. Palmer

STEELE, CURTIS (Popular): Operator 5 Series / Operator 5
    Magazine
  Frederick C. Davis
  Emil Tepperman

STEELE, MORRIS J. (Ziff-Davis)
  Berkley Livingston
  Raymond A. Palmer

STERLING, BRETT (Thrilling): Capt. Future Series / Capt.
    Future Magazine
  Ray Bradbury
  Edmund Hamilton
  Joseph Samachson

STOCKBRIDGE, GRANT (Popular)
  Norvell Page

STODDARD, CHARLES (Thrilling)
  Henry Kuttner

TENNESHAW, S.M. (Ziff-Davis; Greenleaf)
  Randall Garrett
  Chester S. Geier
  Edmund Hamilton
  Milton Lesser
  Charles Nutt
  Robert Silverberg

TOWERS, IVOR (Popular)
  Cyril M. Kornbluth
  Richard Wilson

TOWNE, STEWART (Red Star): Don Diavolo Series / Red Star
    Mystery
  Clayton Rawson

VANCE, GERALD (Ziff-Davis)
  Randall Garrett
  Chester S. Geier
  Roger P. Graham
  Robert Silverberg

WALLACE, ROBERT (Thrilling): Phantom Detective Series / Phantom
    Detective Magazine
  Norman Dannenberg
  G.T. Fleming-Roberts
  Walter Ryerson Johnson

WORTH, PETER (Ziff-Davis)
  Chester S. Geier
  Roger P. Graham

ZIEGFRIED, KARL (BRE)
  Robert Lionel Fanthorpe

ZORRO (Popular): Dr. Death Series / Dr. Death Magazine
  Edward P. Norris
  Harold Ward

SECTION V

STRATEMEYER SYNDICATE NAMES (SSN)

EDWARD L. STRATEMEYER (1862-1930) was an American author and publisher specializing in juvenile adventure-mystery series, with frequent overtones of fantasy and science fiction. Among the series characters he created and developed were such mainstays of children's fiction as Nancy Drew, the Hardy Boys, Tom Swift, Bomba the Jungle Boy, and the Bobbsey Twins. It was Stratemeyer's habit to create the characters of each series and map out the general plots for each book, after which he would either write all or part of each novel or farm the work out to a staff writer. In any case, once an HN was established for a series, it remained unchanged no matter who was doing the writing, over how many years. The SSN Carolyn Keene, used continually for the Nancy Drew series, is an excellent example: Stratemeyer used this name, so did his daughter, Harriet Stratemeyer Adams, and so did Walter Karig, the only other author so far identified in the syndicate with any consistency. In addition to these three, the Keene name was also used by an undetermined number of syndicate writers, some of whom developed plot lines, some of whom wrote alternate chapters of different novels, all of whom are consistent only in their anonymity.

In addition to Stratemeyer, Adams and Karig, it has been established that the following writers worked for the Stratemeyer Syndicate on the following series, among others:

> Lester Dent - Rick Brant Series
> Samuel Epstein - Ken Holt Series
> Howard Garis - Tom Swift Series
> Roger Garis - Outboard Boys Series
> Harold Goodwin - Rick Brant Series
> Leslie McFarlane - Hardy Boys Series
> St. George Rathbone - Camp and Canoe Series; Canoe and
>   Campfire Series; Lend-A-Hand Boys Series; Pioneer Boys
>   Series; Ranch and Range Series

But the breakdown is still far from complete.

ABBOTT, MANAGER HENRY
  Edward L. Stratemeyer

ADAMS, HARRISON
  Edward L. Stratemeyer

APPLETON, VICTOR: Tom Swift Series / Don Sturdy Series
  Howard Garis
  Edward L. Stratemeyer

APPLETON, VICTOR, II: Tom Swift, Jr., Series
  Harriet Stratemeyer Adams

BARNUM, RICHARD

BARTLETT, PHILIP A.

BARTON, MAY HOLLIS
  Harriet Stratemeyer Adams

BEACH, CHARLES AMORY

BLAINE, JOHN: Rick Brant Series
  Lester Dent
  Harold Goodwin
  Peter J. Harkins

BONEHILL, CAPT. RALPH
  Edward L. Stratemeyer

BOWIE, JIM
  Edward L. Stratemeyer

CALKINS, FRANKLIN
  Edward L. Stratemeyer

CHADWICK, LESTER

CHAPMAN, ALLEN
  Edward L. Stratemeyer

CHARLES, LOUIS
  Edward L. Stratemeyer

COOPER, JAMES R.
  Edward L. Stratemeyer

DALY, JIM
  Edward L. Stratemeyer

DAVENPORT, SPENCER: Rushton Boys Series
  Edward L. Stratemeyer

DAWSON, ELMER A.

DIXON, FRANKLIN W.: Hardy Boys Series
  Harriet Stratemeyer Adams
  Leslie McFarlane

DUNCAN, JULIA K.
  Walter Karig

EDWARDS, JULIE
  Edward L. Stratemeyer

EMERSON, ALICE B.: Ruth Felding Series

FERRIS, JAMES CODY: X-Bar-X Boys Series
  Walter Karig

FORBES, GRAHAM B.: Boys of Columbia High Series

FORD, ALBERT LEE
  Edward L. Stratemeyer

GORDON, FREDERICK: Fairview Boys Series

HAMILTON, ROBERT W.
  Edward L. Stratemeyer

HARDY, ALICE DALE

HARKAWAY, HAL
  Edward L. Stratemeyer

HAWLEY, MABEL C.

HENDERLEY, BROOKS

HICKS, HARVEY
  Edward L. Stratemeyer

HILL, GRACE BROOKS: Corner House Girls Series

HOPE, LAURA LEE: Bobbsey Twins Series; Moving Picture Girls
    Series; Bunny Brown Series; Outdoor Girls Series
  Harriet Stratemeyer Adams

HUNT, FRANCIS

JUDD, FRANCES K.

KEENE, CAROLYN: Nancy Drew Series; Dana Girls Series
  Harriet Stratemeyer Adams
  Walter Karig
  Edward L. Stratemeyer

LOCKE, CLINTON W.

LONG, HELEN BEECHER

MacKENZIE, DR. WILLARD

MARLOWE, AMY BELL

MARTIN, EUGENE

MOORE, FENWORTH

MORRISON, GERT W.

PENROSE, MARGARET

RIDLEY, NAT, JR.

ROCKWOOD, ROY: Bomba the Jungle Boy Series
    Edward L. Stratemeyer

ROE, HENRY MASON

ST. MYER, NED
    Edward L. Stratemeyer

SCOTT, DAN: Bret King Series

SHELDON, ANN

SPERRY, RAYMOND, JR.

STEELE, CHESTER K.
    Edward L. Stratemeyer

STONE, ALAN

STONE, RAYMOND

STONE, RICHARD A.

STRAYER, E. WARD
    Edward L. Stratemeyer

THORNDYKE, HELEN LOUISE: Honey Bunch Series; Norman Series
    Harriet Stratemeyer Adams

WARNER, FRANK A.

WEBSTER, FRANK V.: Young Rough Riders Series

WEST, JERRY

WHEELER, JANET D.

WHITE, RAMY ALLISON

WINFIELD, ARTHUR M.: Putnam Hall Series; Rover Boys Series
    Edward L. Stratemeyer

WINFIELD, EDNA
    Edward L. Stratemeyer

WOODS, NAT
    Edward L. Stratemeyer

YOUNG, CLARENCE

APPENDIX A

PULPS & DIGESTS: SOME WORKING DEFINITIONS

The term PULPS properly refers to any magazine printed on pulpwood paper, and usually 7" x 10" in size. Digests also use pulpwood paper, and may be considered something of an outgrowth of Pulps and the Pulp Era, though the forms have always overlapped and, during World War II, both Pulps and Digests coexisted from publisher to publisher.

The term BED-SHEET SIZE refers to any magazine 8½" x 11¼" in size.

The term DIGEST refers to magazines most often 5½" x 8" in size.

The term SLICKS refers to magazines printed on better-grade paper, like that used by the *Saturday Evening Post*, and recently exemplified in the science fiction and fantasy fields by *Vertex*, *Omni* and others. So far the Slicks have met with a mixed acceptance at best.

Nowadays the term "Pulps" is frequently used to describe all of these styles. In the quarter-century since the Pulps expired, memories fade and meanings blur. I have made no attempt to cover the subject in depth, particularly where several fine volumes already exist. However, a very general outline, attempting to place the emergence of different types and styles of publishing in some historical perspective, to help understand the field in general, may not be amiss.

Sometime in the late 1800's, magazines such as the *Atlantic* and *Frank Leslie's* which had used fiction, and the Dime Novels themselves, began to be recognized as portents of a new type of publication. Perhaps the most important and influential of these magazines was *Argosy*, which evolved from a boy's story paper over the first decade of the 20th century to become, by 1910, the first true Pulp. As always, financial considerations were involved. Originally, magazines such as the *Century*, *Scribner's* and the *Atlantic* sold for 25¢ an issue--far out of the reach of the average worker, who made only six or seven dollars for a six-day, ten-hour-a-day work week. *Argosy*, priced at a modest 10¢, climbed to a circulation of 500,000 by 1907, as a weekly magazine with 52 issues per year. Following *Argosy*'s lead, many fine general-fiction magazines appeared, such as *Munsey's*, *All-Story*, *Ocean* and *Blue Book*, but it was not until Oct. 5, 1915, that the first *specialized* Pulp appeared--*Detective Story Magazine*. The format was wildly popular, and other specialized fiction magazines quickly followed: westerns, romances, weird-fantasy with *Weird Tales* in March 1923, and, finally, science fiction with *Amazing Stories* in April 1926. Throughout the following decade it was nearly impossible to have an interest or per-sonal quirk that did not have some Pulp title, somewhere, devoted to it.

With the advent of *Reader's Digest* in 1921, a new, poten-tially acceptable format was added to the publishers' output, even though, in the fiction field, there were few attempts at this new form until World War II. *Marvel Tales* for May, July-August and Winter 1934, and March-April 1935, and *Unusual Stories* for April-May and Winter 1935, were issued in semi-Digest size, but these had only limited circulation and, while excellent in content, were not well received by fandom and the readers of the time. Hugo Gernsbach, who had created *Amazing Stories*, also published a long series of Digest-size pamphlets, but as all of these were available for years after their initial publication, it may be safely assumed that they were not well received originally. It must be stressed at this time that *content* was not in question: it was purely a matter of *size*. The 7" x 10" Pulp had achieved universal recognition as the "proper," "classic" size for fiction maga-zines, and it was apparently unthinkable that any other maga-zine size would be tolerated, no matter how high the magazine's standards, or how outré its subject matter.

Gernsbach had not only created the science fiction Pulp, he had also created science fiction fandom, partly by acci-dent, evolving as it did quite naturally out of the readers' columns of his magazines. He would run long letters uncut, complete with names and addresses, and it was only common sense to group the letters and the letter writers according to mutual interests in his publications. Thus a natural forum for readers was created, and quickly shaped itself into a fan club (The Science Fiction League), which, through its interests and demands, led directly to the further development of the science fiction field in all its written forms. Gernsbach also ran contests to help develop new authors in the field.

Pulp magazines were not all clear-cut and departmentalized, of course: there were many hybrids. *Witch's Tales* for Nov. and Dec. 1936 expanded to Bed-sheet size, as did the Dec. 1936 issue of *Flash Gordon Strange Adventures Magazine*. Also, a number of Gernsbach's magazines were originally Bed-sheet,

later changing over to Pulp size. The Bed-sheet format was
also used by *Fantastic Adventures*, starting with May 1939,
through May 1940. Another fascinating hybrid was *Stirring
Science Stories* for Feb., April and June 1941, and March 1942.
This was actually two Pulp magazines in one, the first 60
pages devoted to science fiction, the second 60 pages to fantasy. There was also a half-detective and half-western magazine. All of these hybrids are now classed as Pulps, despite
their variations in size.

     With the advent of World War II, and the ensuing paper
shortages, many magazines limited their schedules, skipped
issues, changed over to the suddenly acceptable Digest size
(as did the venerable and respected *Astounding Stories*, with
its Nov. 1943 issue), or folded outright. The war years gave
a sudden legitimate standing to many new formats. There were
a few experiments with Pocket-size magazines which were
actually miniature Digests; more and more actual Digests
appeared, and Avon pioneered both in format and content with
the *Avon Fantasy Reader*. Pocket series became more common,
particularly after Pocket Books led off with *Lost Horizon*, a
romance-fantasy published in May 1939 (Pocket series had
appeared intermittently before 1939, but this was the first
time they had been allowed fine titles, a large budget, and
wide circulation.)

     Basically, the Pulp-Digest conflict was one of physical
convenience, and though Digests and Pocket books did not have
the mystique and readership identification of the Pulps, they
were easier to mail out to G.I.'s and easier for the soldiers
to carry in pockets or packs. The Armed Service Editions
were specifically designed to be carried in uniform pockets.
This fact provided an enormous impetus for the burgeoning
Paperback field, and after the War rising paper costs, falter-
ing distributorships and printing increases left Paperback
books and Digests firmly entrenched in the public awareness.
Another fact was discovered: Paperbacks, bearing numbers
rather than dates, could be displayed for longer periods of
time than dated Pulps, and the smaller sizes allowed more
display space for the retailer.

     As a viable publishing format, Pulps may be said to have
given up the ghost in April-May 1953, when *Amazing Stories*
finally changed from Pulp to Digest size (its sister magazine,
Fantastic Adventures, had folded with the March 1953 issue).
Some Pulps straggled on for a few more issues, and the western
Pulps seem to have been the last to go under. At the height
of their popularity, in the early '60's, three television
shows, "Tightrope," "77 Sunset Strip" and "Wagon Train" had
newsstand-distributed Pulp counterparts, and in 1973-1974 for
its 4-issue run the revived *Weird Tales* tried a slim, neat

Pulp format, but the era was over, and all of these attempts
petered out quickly.

A word about foreign publications: The output in America
throughout the Pulp Era and into the continuing Paperback/
Digest Era has been so enormous that many readers still assume
that any or all foreign editions can only be pirated translations of original American works. However, the creativity
has been at least as intense, if not as immense over as long
a period of time, in Europe as in America, and overseas
magazines have appeared in all imaginable formats. Argentina's
Narraciones Terrorificas was a beautifully produced Pulp;
Sweden's *Jules Verne Magazinet* was in format like our comic
books; England has produced Pulps (often British editions of
U.S. magazines), slim Digests, Paperbacks and pamphlets distributed as magazines. Canada produced Pulps generally close
to the American products; Australia has done everything from
pamphlets to neat Digests; Mexico has done mainly Digests, or
slim magazine-pamphlets, such as *Los Curentos Fantasticos*;
and Germany, to mention only its most recent format, seems to
have the continuing-modern serial-hero format sewn up with
its *Perry Rhodan* series.

APPENDIX B

ROUND ROBIN SERIALS (RR)

Although the serial concept of novel writing had been in
existence, one way or the other, since the beginnings of the
story papers, it was left to the science fiction authors to
carry the concept one step further, and create a separate
sub-phenomenon, still fondly remembered as the Round Robins.
Basically, one writer would start the ball rolling by writing
a first chapter, then pass the manuscript on for a second
chapter to a second writer, and so on. Presumably, some sort
of basic (in some cases, subliminal) plot line was prearranged,
though no chapter writer need feel completely bound to the
exigencies of plot, and could develop characters, story twists
and separate writing styles to the furthest extent of imagina-
tion, so long as he left something hanging for the next writer
to tack the next chapter on. Since professional writers were
involved, the theory was an interesting one, and the results,
while complex, could not be dismissed as amateurish, but the
whole mode of creation was such an editor's nightmare, depend-
ing on so many different writers to settle down and create one
story, that perhaps not surprisingly, the phenomenon blossomed
and faded as abruptly as a night-blooming cereus. Because of
the authors involved, however, a breakdown of the known Round
Robins is still of interest and value.

(A) COSMO, *Science Fiction Digest*, *Fantasy Magazine*, c. early
    to mid-1930's. This was the first of the RR's, and still
    stands as the best ever produced, since each of its 17
    chapters can also stand as a separate short story, and
    several have become minor classics of the genre. Contrib-
    uting writers were:

    Eando Binder
    Arthur J. Burke
    John W. Campbell, Jr.
    Lloyd Arthur Eshbach
    Ralph Milne Farley

Francis Flagg
Abner J. Geula
J. Harvey Haggard
Edmund Hamilton
David H. Keller
Otis Adelbert Kline
A. Merritt
P. Schuyler Miller
Bob Olsen
Ray Palmer
E. Hoffman Price
E.E. Smith
Rae Winters

COSMO has since been serialized in the U.S. edition of
Perry Rhodan, and in 1978 was announced as a forthcoming,
separate book.

(B) THE MOON DOOM, *Wonder Stories*, Feb. 1933–June 1933, 4 parts.

Part 1: Nathaniel Salisbury   WS 1933 Feb.
Part 2: William Lichtenstein   WS 1933 Apr.
Part 3: Wesley P. Baird   WS 1933 May
Part 4: Clinton Earle Fisk   WS 1933 June

(C) CHALLENGE FROM BEYOND 1 & 2, *Fantasy Magazine*, 3rd anni-
versary issue, c. 1935. Basically, CHALLENGE was two
separate stories, Part 1 being Science Fiction and Part 2,
Fantasy. Only the Lovecraft segment in Part 2 stands as
a separate story, although, when read as a whole, both
parts are better than average.

Part 1: Science Fiction
   Stanley G. Weinbaum
   Donald Wandrei
   Edward E. Smith
   Murray Leinster
   Harl Vincent

Part 2: Fantasy
   A. Merritt
   C.L. Moore
   H.P. Lovecraft
   Robert E. Howard
   Frank Belknap Long

(D) THE PRESIDENT'S MYSTERY STORY, *Liberty Magazine*, Nov.
1935. Hardbound editions published by Farrar & Rinehart
1935, Lane 1936 and P-H 1967. This is the star of the
RR's, as the plot was supplied by no less a celebrity than

Franklin Delano Roosevelt (which fact may also account
for the subsequent hardbound editions). Various chapters
were written in succession by:

Rupert Hughes
Samuel Hopkins Adams
Rita Weiman
S.S. Van Dyne
John Erskine
Fulton Oursler (writing as Anthony Abbott)

(E) THE GREAT ILLUSION, *Fantasy Magazine*, Sept. 1936.

Eando Binder
Jack Williamson
Edmund Hamilton
Raymond Z. Gallun
John Russell Fearn

SOURCES & REFERENCES

Anonymous. DUENDE 2, Odyssey Publications 1977, Greenwood, Mass. 01880.

Anonymous. INDEX TO PERRY RHODAN, U.S. edition, Vol. 1: 1-25; Vol. 2: 26-50, NESFA (New England Science Fiction Assn.) 1975, Cambridge, Mass. 02139.

Anonymous. INDEX TO THE SCIENCE FICTION MAGAZINES: 1966-1970, NESFA 1971, Cambridge, Mass. 02139.

Anonymous. THE NESFA INDEX: 1971-1972, NESFA 1973, Cambridge, Mass. 02139.

Anonymous. THE NESFA INDEX: 1973, NESFA 1974, Cambridge, Mass. 02139.

Anonymous. THE NESFA INDEX: 1974, NESFA 1975, Cambridge, Mass. 02139.

Anonymous. THE NESFA INDEX: 1975, NESFA 1976, Cambridge, Mass. 02139.

Anonymous. THE NESFA INDEX: 1976, NESFA 1977, Cambridge, Mass. 02139.

Anonymous. ODYSSEY PRESS 10, Odyssey Publications 1977, Greenwood, Mass. 01880.

Bleiler, E.F. THE CHECKLIST OF SCIENCE-FICTION & SUPERNATURAL FICTION, Firebell Press 1978, Glenrock, N.J. 07452.

Brooks, C.W. THE REVISED HANNES BOK CHECKLIST, T-K Graphics 1974, Baltimore, Md. 21203.

Brown, Charles (Ed.). LOCUS, Vol. 1: 1968-1971; Vol. 2: 1972-1977, Gregg Press 1978, Boston, Mass. 02111.

Cockcroft, T.G.L. INDEX TO FICTION IN RADIO NEWS & OTHER MAGAZINES, 1970, Lower Hutt, New Zealand.

Cockcroft, T.G.L. INDEX TO THE VERSE IN WEIRD TALES, 1960, Lower Hutt, New Zealand.

Cockcroft, T.G.L. INDEX TO THE WEIRD FICTION MAGAZINES, Vols.
    1 & 2, 1967, Lower Hutt, New Zealand.

Crawford, Joseph H. 333: A BIBLIOGRAPHY OF THE SCIENCE-FANTASY
    NOVEL, Grandon 1953, Providence, R.I. 02905.

Day, Donald. INDEX TO THE SCIENCE FICTION MAGAZINES: 1926-
    1950, Perri Press 1952, Portland, Ore. 97208.

Derleth, August (Ed.). THE ARKHAM COLLECTOR, Nos. 1-10,
    Summer 1967-Summer 1971, Sauk City, Wisc. 53583.

Derleth, August. THIRTY YEARS OF ARKHAM HOUSE: 1939-1969,
    Arkham House 1970, Sauk City, Wisc. 53583.

Engin, Orrin A. WRITER OF THE PLAINS: A BIOGRAPHY OF B.M.
    BOWER, Pontine Press 1973, Culver City, Cal. 90230.

Gibson, Walter B. THE SHADOW SCRAPBOOK, Harcourt Brace
    Jovanovich, Inc. 1979, New York, N.Y. 10017.

Goodstone, Tony (Ed.). THE PULPS, Chelsea House 1970, New
    York, N.Y. 10018.

Goulart, Ron. INFORMAL HISTORY OF THE PULP MAGAZINE (Original
    title, CHEAP THRILLS), Ace 1973, New York, N.Y. 10036.

Gruber, Frank. THE PULP JUNGLE, Sherbourne Press 1967, Los
    Angeles, Cal. 90035.

Hagen, Ordean A. WHO DONE IT?, R.R. Bowker Co. 1969, New
    York, N.Y. 10036.

Hudson, Harry K. A BIBLIOGRAPHY OF HARD-COVER, SERIES-TYPE
    BOYS' BOOKS, privately published 1978, Inverness, Fla.
    32650.

Jones, Bob. THE SHUDDER PULPS, Plume 1975, New York, N.Y.
    10019.

Jones, Bob. THE WEIRD MENACE, Opar Press 1972, Evergreen,
    Colo. 80439.

Lovecraft, H.P. SELECTED LETTERS OF HPL: Vol. 1, 1911-1924;
    Vol. 2, 1925-1929; Vol. 3, 1929-1931; Vol. 4, 1932-1934;
    Vol. 5, 1935-1937, Arkham House 1965- , Sauk City, Wisc.
    53583.

Lovecraft, H.P. SUPERNATURAL HORROR IN LITERATURE, Dover
    1973, New York, N.Y. 10014.

Lundwall, Sam J. SCIENCE FICTION: WHAT IT'S ALL ABOUT, Ace
    1971, New York, N.Y. 10036.

Lupoff, Richard. EDGAR RICE BURROUGHS, MASTER OF ADVENTURE,
    Ace 1968, New York, N.Y. 10036.

Metcalf, Norm. INDEX TO THE SCIENCE FICTION MAGAZINES: 1951-1965, J. Ben Stark Publications 1968, El Cerrito, Cal. 94530.

Morse, A. Reynolds. THE WORKS OF M.P. SHIEL, FPCI 1948, Alhambra, Cal. 91801.

Moskowitz, Sam. THE IMMORTAL STORM: A HISTORY OF SCIENCE FICTION FANDOM, Hyperion Press 1974, Westport, Conn. 06880.

Moskowitz, Sam, & Seiger, James R. GHOST STORIES INDEX, Opar Press 1973, Evergreen, Colo. 80439.

Mott, Frank Luther. GOLDEN MULTITUDES, Macmillan 1947, New York, N.Y. 10022.

Reynolds, Quentin. THE FICTION FACTORY, Random House 1955, New York, N.Y. 10022.

Sharp, Harold S. HANDBOOK OF PSEUDONYMS & PERSONAL NICKNAMES, Vols. 1 & 2, Scarecrow Press 1972, Metuchen, N.J. 08840.

Sharp, Harold S. SUPPLEMENT to the above, Vols. 1 & 2, Scarecrow Press 1972, Metuchen, N.J. 08840.

Steinbrunner, Chris, & Penzler, Otto. ENCYCLOPEDIA OF MYSTERY & DETECTION, McGraw-Hill 1976, New York, N.Y. 10036.

Stone, Graham. AUSTRALIAN SCIENCE FICTION INDEX: 1925-1967, ASFA 1968, Canberra, Australia.

Stone, Graham. ASFA SUPPLEMENT: 1968-1975, ASFA 1976, Canberra, Australia.

Stone, Graham. INDEX TO BRITISH SCIENCE FICTION MAGAZINES: 1934-1953, Vol. 1, ASFA 1977, Sydney, Australia.

Theissen, J. Grant. THE SCIENCE FICTION COLLECTOR, Nos. 1-6, Theissen Publisher 1976-1978, Calgary, Alberta, Canada.

Tuck, Donald H. THE ENCYCLOPEDIA OF SCIENCE FICTION & FANTASY, Vol. 1, A-L, Advent 1974; Vol. 2, M-Z, Advent 1978, Chicago, Ill. 60690.

Warner, Harry, Jr. ALL OUR YESTERDAYS, Advent 1969, Chicago, Ill. 60690.

Weinberg, Robert (Ed.). WEIRD TALES COLLECTOR Nos. 1-4, Weinberg Publisher 1978, Chicago, Ill. 60655.

Weinberg, Robert, & McKinstry, L. THE HERO PULP INDEX, Opar Press 1971, Evergreen, Colo. 80439.

Wentz, W. James. A. MERRITT: A BIBLIOGRAPHY OF FANTASTIC WRITINGS, Geo A. Bibby 1965, Roseville, Cal. 95678.

INDEX

Real Names are listed in capital letters. The
first page reference for each entry is to the
principal section in which the name appears.

A, Dr.: PN 71, 5
A.L.O.E.: PN 71, 63
AARONS, EDWARD S. 3, 75, 127
Abbott, Anthony: PN 71, 48, 173
ABBOTT, EDWIN A. 3, 133
Abbott, Manager Henry: SSN 164
Abdullah, Achmed: PN 71, 54
ABRAHAMSEN, CHRISTINE 3, 87
ACKERMAN, FORREST J. 3, 71, 72, 75, 76, 93, 107, 111, 116,
    118, 119, 125, 134, 137, 139, 140, 142, 146
Acre, Stephen: PN 71, 30
Acula, Dr.: PN 3, 71
Adair, Dennis: PN 71, 17
ADAMS, CLEVE FRANKLIN 4, 83, 132
ADAMS, HARRIET STRATEMEYER 4, 164, 165, 166
Adams, Harrison: SSN 164
ADAMS, HERBERT 4, 99
ADAMS, J. 4, 108
Adams, Jack: PN 71, 30
ADAMS, SAMUEL HOPKINS 4, 173
ADAMS, WILLIAM T. 4, 74, 80, 105, 112, 120, 142
Addison, Hugh: PN 71, 48,
Addy, Ted: PN 71, 68
Adeler, Max: PN 71, 14
Adept, An: PN 71, 36
AE: PN 71, 54
Agar, Brian: PN 72, 5
Aghill, Gordon: HN 151, 27, 57
Agricola, Sylvius: PN 72, 3
Aguecheek: PN 72, 23
Ahearne, Burt: PN 72, 33
Ainsbury, Ray: PN 72, 63
Aird, Catherine: PN 72, 43

Buckrose, J.E.: PN 80, 35
BUDRYS, ALGEDRAS JONAS 11, 80, 106
Budrys, Algis: PN 80, 11
BULMER, (Henry) KENNETH 11, 86, 101, 107, 114, 131, 143,
    147, 156
BULWER-LYTTON, EDWARD ROBERT 11, 113
Buntline, Ned: PN 80, 36
Burford, Eleanor: PN 80, 33
Burgess, Anthony: PN 81, 67
Burke, Ralph: HN 153, 27, 57
BURKHILDER, EDWIN 11, 157
BURKITT, FREDERICK 12, 148
BURK, ARTHUR J. 12, 171, 87, 111, 141
Burns, Tex: HN 153, 38
BURRAGE, ALFRED McCLELLAND 12, 143
BURROUGHS, EDGAR RICE 12, 76, 112
BURROUGHS, WILLIAM S. 12, 110
BURTON, ELIZABETH J. 12, 108
Burton, Miles: PN 81, 60
BUTLER, SAMUEL 12, 121
Butler, Walter G.: PN 81, 23
Buxton, Carl: PN 81, 33
Buzz-Bolt Atomcracker: PN 81, 67
BYRNE, STUART JAMES 12, 78, 88, 107

Cabell, Branch: PN 81, 12
CABELL, JAMES BRANCH 12, 81
Cabot, John York: PN 81, 47
Caine, Geff: PN 81, 54
Cairnes, Maud: PN 81, 17
Calkins, Franklin: SSN 164
Callahan, William: PN 81, 26
Cameron, Ian: PN 81, 49, 68
Campbell, Clyde Crain: PN 81, 28
CAMPBELL, GABRIELLE 12, 79, 130
Campbell, Hope: PN 81, 64
CAMPBELL, JOHN W(ood), JR. 12, 172, 81, 112, 134
Campbell, R.T.: PN 81, 62
Campen, Karl van: PN 81, 12
Cannon, Curt: PN 81, 40
CAPPS, CARROLL M. 12, 112
Caraman, Georges: PN 81, 58
Cardinal, Jane: PN 81, 67
Carghill, Ralph: PN 81, 16
Carleton, H.B.: HN 153, 11
Carlisle, Clark: PN 82, 34
Carnac, Carol: PN 82, 153
CARR, JOHN DICKSON 12, 90

Dean, Paul: PN 89, 26
Deane, Norman: PN 89, 16
Dearborn, Laura: PN 89, 50
De BANZIE, ERIC 18, 145
Debrett, Hal: CPN 145, 21, 54
De BURY, F. BLAZE 18, 90
De CAMP, L(yon) SPRAGUE 18, 111, 140
De Costa, Henry: PN 89, 51
Dee, Roger: PN 89, 5
DEEPING, GEORGE WARWICK 18, 89, 139
Deeping, Warwick: PN 89, 18
Deer, M.J.: CPN 146, 18, 59
DEER, M. JANE 18, 146
De FOIGNY, GABRIEL 19, 128
Degen, Von: PN 89, 51
De Graeff, W.B.: PN 89, 15
Dehan, Richard: PN 89, 29
De KREMER, RAYMOND 19, 95, 124
de la MARE, WALTER 19, 124
Dell, Dudley: PN 89, 28
Del Martia, Astron: PN 89, 24
Delorme, Charles: PN 89, 54
del REY, LESTER 19, 23, 72, 100, 102, 106, 128, 138, 147, 160
De MATTOS, MRS. 19, 102
De MELIKOFF, JODI 19, 147
Demijohn, Thom: CPN 146, 20, 58
Deming, Kirk: PN 89, 21
Denholm, Mark: PN 89, 24
Dennis, Bruce: PN 89, 47
DENNIS, WALTER 19, 147
DENT, LESTER 19, 82, 128, 156, 159, 163, 164
Dentinger, Stephen: PN 89, 33
Denver, Drake C.: PN 90, 47
De PATOT, SIMON TYSSOT 19, 115
De Pre, Jean-Anne: PN 90, 5
DERLETH, AUGUST 19, 99, 115, 140
Dersonne, Jacques: PN 90, 58
de St. Leon, Count Reginald: PN 90, 21
D'Esme, Jean: PN 90, 19
D'ESMENARD, JEAN 19, 90
Devereux, Roy: PN 90, 49
De WEASE, GENE 19, 149
De WEINDECK, WINTELER 19, 94
DeWreder, Paul: PN 90, 32
Dexter, Martin: PN 90, 24
Dexter, William: PN 90, 51
DEY, F. VAN RENSSELAER 20, 153

MAINWARING, DANIEL 43, 104
Majors, Simon: PN 113, 26
Malcolm, Dan: PN 113, 57
Malet, Lucas: PN 113, 32
Malet, Oriel: PN 113, 63
Mallik, B.K.: PN 113, 30
MALZBURG, BARRY 43, 119
Manasco, Norman: PN 113, 30
Mann, Abel: PN 114, 16
MANN, GEORGE 43, 152
Mann, Jack: PN 114, 64
Mann, Milton: HN 158, 29
MANNING, ADELAIDE F.O. 43, 145, 146
Manning, David: PN 114, 24
Man of the People, A: PN 114, 61
Manton, Peter: PN 114, 16
Maras, Karl: PN 114, 11
Mariner, Scott: PN 114, 37
Mark, Ted: PN 114, 29
Markham, Robert: PN 114, 4
Marlowe, Amy Bell: SSN 165
Marlowe, Louis: PN 114, 67
Marlowe, Stephen: PN 114, 39
Marlowe, Webb: PN 114, 42
Marric, J.J.: PN 114, 16
Marsden, Anthony: PN 114, 61
MARSH, JOHN 44, 93, 101, 125, 142
MARSHALL, EDISON (Tesla) 44, 105
Marshall, James Vance: PN 114, 49
Marshall, Raymond: PN 114, 52
Marsten, Richard: PN 114, 40
Martens, Paul: PN 114, 59
Martin, Eugene: SSN 165
MARTIN, F.H. 44, 158
Martin, Ken: PN 114, 34
MARTIN, R.A. 44, 92
Martin, Richard: PN 115, 16
Martin, Sam: PN 115, 46
MARTIN, THOMAS HECTOR 44, 136, 160
Martin, Webber: PN 115, 57
MARTYN, EDWARD 44, 131
Martyn, Philip: PN 115, 62
Marvell, Andrew: PN 115, 18
MASON, C.P. 44, 132
MASON, DOUGLAS 44, 124
MASON, F(rancis) VAN WYCK 44, 140, 115, 84
Mason, Frank W.: PN 115, 44
Mason, Gregory: CPN 147, 36, 44

Nader, Seena: PN 118, 3
naGopaleen, Myles: PN 118, 48
Nathan, Daniel: PN 118, 17
Navarchus: CPN 148, 63, 69
Neal, Favin: PN 118, 62
Neal, Harry: PN 118, 9
Nemo, Omen: PN 118, 52
Netterfield, Luke: PN 118, 48
Netterville, Luke: PN 118, 48
Netzen, Klaus: PN 118, 35
NEVILLE, KRIS 46, 133
Newman, A.: PN 118, 50
NEWMAN, BERNARD 46, 77
NEWMAN, JOHN 47, 147
Newman, Robert: PN 118, 47
Nichols, Scott: PN 118, 55
Nicholson, John: PN 118, 49
NICOLL, MAURICE 47, 135
Nihil: PN 118, 45
Nile, Dorothea: PN 118, 5
NISOT, MRS. MAVIS E. 47, 122
Noel, L.: PN 118, 6
Nolan, Christopher: PN 118, 35
Noname: PN 118, 56
Noone, Edwina: PN 119, 5
Norbert, W.: PN 119, 67
Norfolk, William: PN 119, 23
Norman, John: PN 119, 38
Normyx: PN 119, 38
NORRIS, EDWARD P. 47, 161
North, Andrew: PN 119, 47
North, Eric: PN 119, 17
Northen, Leslie: PN 119, 40
NORTHRUP, EDWIN F. 47, 123
NORTON, ALICE MARY 47, 119, 140
Norton, Andre: PN 119, 47
NORTON, ROGER HOWARD 47, 78, 118
NORWAY, NEVIL SHUTE 47, 131
Nostradamus, Merlin: PN 119, 14
Notte, Astrid: PN 119, 3
NOWLAN, PHILIP FRANCIS 47, 122
NUETZEL, CHARLES ALXANDER 47, 93
NUTT, CHARLES 47, 76, 99, 111, 113, 161
Nuverbis: PN 119, 59
NYE, NELSON CORAL 47, 84, 90, 126

O'BRIEN, DAVID WRIGHT 47, 81, 89, 94, 138, 152, 156
O'Brien, Dean D.: CPN 148, 8

Padgett, Lewis: CPN 148, 38, 46
Page, Marco: PN 121, 38
PAGE, NORVELL 48, 155, 160
PAGET, VIOLET 49, 110
Paget-Lowe, Henry: PN 121, 41
Pain, Barry: PN 121, 48
PAINE, LAUREN 49, 110
Palinurus: PN 122, 15
PALMER, (Charles) STUART 49, 120, 134
PALMER, JOHN LESLIE 49, 145
PALMER, RAYMOND A. 49, 172, 122, 124, 140, 142, 156, 157,
    159, 160
PALTOCK, ROBERT 49, 128
Pan: PN 121, 8
PANGBORN, EDGAR 49, 101
Parabellum: PN 121, 29
Paradice, Mary: PN 121, 21
PARCELL, NORMAN H. 49, 118
PARGETER, EDITH 49, 122
Paris, John: PN 121, 5
Park, Jordan: CPN 148, 37, 51
Parkes, Wyndham: PN 121, 31
Parr, Robert: PN 121, 27
Partridge, Anthony: PN 121, 48
PARTRIDGE, EDWARD BELLAMY 49, 75
Passante, Dom: PN 121, 24
Patrick, Keats: PN 121, 36
Patrick, Q.: CPN 148, 65, 66
Patriot, A: PN 121, 31
PATTEN, LEWIS BYFORD 49, 95
PATTEN, WILLIAM GILBERT 49, 148
Patton, Frank: HN 159, 49, 56
PAYES, RACHEL COSGROVE 49, 73
PAYNE, DONALD GORDON 49, 81, 98, 114
Payne, Guthrie: PN 121, 62
Payton, Green: PN 122, 66
Pearson, Martin: PN 122, 68
Pease, Lt. John: PN 122, 33
Peccavi: PN 122, 30
Peddiwell, J. Abner: PN 122, 8
Pelkie, Joe W(alter): PN 122, 49
PEMBER-DEVEREUX, MARGARET R. 49, 90
Pendarves, G.G.: PN 122, 62
PENDLETON, DON 50, 99
PENDRAY, EDWARD 50, 92
Penmare, William: PN 122, 47
Penrose, Margaret: SSN 166
Pentecost, Hugh: PN 122, 50

Stone, Raymond: SSN 166
Stone, Richard A.: SSN 166
Storm, Harrison: PN 134, 25
Storm, Russell: PN 67, 134
STORY, A.M. SOMMERVILLE 60, 132
STOWE, MRS. H.M. 60, 92
Strang, Herbert: CPN 148, 22, 39
STRATEMEYER, EDWARD L. 60, 164, 165, 166
Stratton, Thomas: CPN 148, 16, 19
Strayer, E. Ward: SSN 166
STREET, CECIL JOHN CHARLES 60, 81, 94, 125, 143
Stringer, David: PN 134, 53
Strong, Harrington: PN 134, 42
Strong, Spenser: PN 134, 3
Stuart, Clay: PN 66, 134
Stuart, Don A.: PN 134, 12
Stuart, Ian: PN 134, 43
Stuart, Sidney: PN 134, 5
STUBBS, HARRY CLEMENT 60, 84
Student of Occultism, A: PN 135, 32
STURGEON, THEODORE 60, 94, 105, 139
SUDDABY, WILLIAM DONALD 60, 100
Sutter, Philip: PN 135, 60
SUTTON, GRAHAM 61, 114
SWAIN, DWIGHT V(reeland) 61, 132
Swanson, Logan: PN 135, 44
Swayne, Martin: PN 135, 47
Sweven, Godfrey: PN 135, 11
Swift, Anthony: PN 135, 23
Swift, Augustus T.: PN 135, 41
SWIFT, JONATHAN 61, 77, 100
SWINTON, SIR ERNEST DUNLOP 61, 120
SYMMES, JOHN CLEAVES 61, 129

Taine, John: PN 135, 8
TAIT, GEORGE B. 69, 75
Tangent, Patrick Q.: PN 135, 50
Tarnacre, Robert: PN 135, 13
Tate, Ellalice: PN 135, 33
Taverel, John: PN 135, 34
Taylor, Bruce: PN 135, 40
TAYLOR, PHOEBE ATWOOD 61, 136
TEED, C(yrus) R(eed) 61, 83
Temple, James: PN 135, 8
Temple-Ellis, N.A.: PN 135, 34
Tenn, William: PN 135, 37
Tenneshaw, S.M.: HN 161, 27, 31, 39, 47, 58
TEPPERMAN, EMIL 61, 159, 160

TRACY, LOUIS   62, 146
TRACY, ROGER S.   62, 103
Traprock, Walter E.: PN 137, 14
Traven, B.: PN 137, 62
Traver, Robert: PN 137, 64
TREMAINE, F. ORLIN   62, 76, 109, 121, 129, 138
TRENERY, GLADYS GORDON   62, 122
Trent, Clyve: PN 137, 22
Trevena, John: PN 137, 32
TREVOR, ELLESTON   62, 100
Trout, Kilgore: PN 137, 23
TUBB, E(dwin) C(harles)   62, 75, 99, 100, 104, 108, 109, 113,
     115, 118, 130, 131, 152, 157
TUCKER, CHARLOTTE   63, 71
TUCKER, GEORGE   63, 74
TUCKER, NATHANIEL BEVERLEY   63, 131
Turbojew, Alexai: PN 137, 55
Twain, Mark: PN 137, 14
Two Wags: CPN 149, 6, 56
Tyler, Theodore: PN 137, 69
Tyson, Arnold: PN 137, 33

Underwood, Michael: PN 137, 22
UNWIN, DAVID STORR   63, 130
UPCHURCH, BOYD   63, 79
Uriel, Henry: PN 137, 24
Usher, Margo Seesse: PN 138, 43

Vaeth, Martin: PN 138, 37
VAIRASSE, DENIS   63, 131
Valding, Victor: PN 138, 8
Valentine, Jo: PN 138, 4
Vance, Geoffrey: PN 138, 13
Vance, Gerold: HN 161, 27, 29, 58
Vance, Jack: PN 138, 63
VANCE, JOHN HOLBROOK   63, 138
VANCEL, DORIS   63, 136
Van Dine, S.S.: PN 138, 173, 69
Van Dyne, Edith: PN 138, 7
Van Lhin, Erik: PN 138, 19
Van Lorne, Warner: PN 138, 62
Vanshuck, Grego: PN 138, 28
Vara, Madeleine: PN 138, 53
Vardon, Richard: PN 138, 47
VAUGHAN, AURIEL R.   63, 113
VAUX, PATRICK   63, 148
Vedder, John K.: PN 138, 30
Vellin, Edward J.: PN 138, 38